Title: "the money mastery: Unlocking the Secrets to Financial Abundance"

Chapter 1: Understanding Your Financial Landscape

- Assessing Your Current Financial Situation
- Setting Clear Financial Goals
- Identifying Your Spending Habits and Patterns

Chapter 2: Building A Solid Financial Foundation

- Creating a Realistic Budget
- Emergency Fund Essentials: Why It's Crucial and How to Start
- Debunking Common Money Myths

Chapter 3: Mastering Mindful Spending

- Differentiating Between Needs and Wants
- Practicing Delayed Gratification Techniques
- Harnessing the Power of Budgeting Apps and Tools

Chapter 4: Maximizing Savings Through Smart Shopping

- Strategies for Strategic Shopping: Coupons, Sales, and Discounts
- Comparison Shopping: Finding the Best Deals
- Avoiding Impulse Purchases and Buyer's Remorse

Chapter 5: Supercharging Your Savings With Frugal Living

- Embracing Minimalism: Simplifying Your Lifestyle
- DIY: Saving Money by Doing It Yourself
- Repurposing and Upcycling: Finding Value in the Everyday

Chapter 6: Investing In Your Future

- Exploring Different Investment Options: Stocks, Bonds, Real Estate, and more
- Understanding Risk and Return: Building a Diversified Investment Portfolio
- Starting Small: How to Begin Investing with Limited Funds

Chapter 7: Navigating Financial Challenges

- Dealing with Debt: Strategies for Repayment and Avoidance
- Overcoming Financial Hurdles: Job Loss, Medical Emergencies, and Unexpected Expenses
- Seeking Professional Help: When and How to Consult Financial Advisors

Chapter 8: Cultivating Long-Term Financial Success

- Setting and Reviewing Financial Milestones
- Practicing Consistency and Discipline
- Celebrating Your Financial Victories: Rewarding Yourself Without Breaking the Bank

Chapter 9: Passing Down Wealth Wisdom

- Teaching Financial Literacy to Children and Young Adults
- Inculcating Healthy Money Mindsets and Habits in the Next Generation
- Leaving a Legacy: Estate Planning and Charitable Giving

Epilogue: Your Journey to Financial Freedom
- Reflecting on Your Progress
- Committing to Lifelong Learning and Improvement
- Empowering Others: Sharing Your Knowledge and Experience

Throughout the book, readers will find practical tips, real-life examples, and actionable steps to help them save money effectively and build a secure financial future. "The Money Mastery" is not just a guide; it's a companion for anyone seeking to achieve financial independence and peace of mind.

Acknowledgment:

Writing a book like the "the money mastery" is a collaborative effort that involves the contributions and support of many individuals and organizations. As such, I would like to express my sincere gratitude and appreciation to everyone who has played a part in bringing this project to fruition.

First and foremost, I would like to thank Jennifer whose expertise, insights, and dedication have been instrumental in shaping the content of this book. Your passion for personal finance and commitment to empowering others shines through in every chapter, and I am grateful for the opportunity to collaborate with you on this project.

I would also like to extend my heartfelt thanks to the team, including the editors, designers, and production staff, for their hard work and professionalism in bringing this book to life. Your attention to detail, creativity, and dedication to quality have ensured that the "The Money Mastery" meets the highest standards of excellence.

I am deeply grateful to the individuals who generously shared their time, expertise, and personal stories for inclusion in this book. Your insights and experiences have added depth and authenticity to the content, and I am honored to have had the opportunity to feature your contributions.

I would also like to thank my family and friends for their unwavering support and encouragement throughout the writing process. Your love, patience, and understanding have been a source of strength and inspiration, and I am truly grateful for your presence in my life.

Last but not least, I want to express my gratitude to the readers of the "The Money Mastery." It is my sincere hope that this book will empower you with the knowledge, skills, and confidence to achieve your financial goals and create a life of abundance and fulfillment. Thank you for embarking on this journey with us.

With deepest appreciation,

[Kenneth Christopher]

Introduction:

In a world where financial uncertainty looms large and economic landscapes shift with the changing winds, the quest for financial security has become more than just a pursuit—it's a necessity. Yet, amidst the cacophony of conflicting advice and the allure of instant gratification, the path to financial stability often seems shrouded in mystery, an enigma waiting to be unraveled.

But fear not, for within the pages of this book lies the beacon of hope, the roadmap to prosperity, and the key to unlocking the doors of financial freedom. Welcome to "The Money Mastery: Unlocking the Secrets to Financial Abundance."

In the bustling market place of personal finance literature, this book stands apart as a beacon of clarity and practicality. Drawing upon timeless principles and cutting-edge strategies, "The Money

Mastery" is not just another guide to saving money—it's your trusted companion on the journey to financial empowerment.

Picture this: You wake up each morning, not with a sense of dread about your financial future, but with a renewed sense of purpose and direction. With each penny saved and each dollar invested wisely, you inch closer to your dreams—a comfortable retirement, a debt-free existence, and the freedom to pursue your passions without constraint.

But before we embark on this transformative journey together, let us pause to reflect on the power of choice. For in the realm of personal finance, every decision—no matter how seemingly insignificant—has the potential to shape our financial destiny. Will you succumb to the siren call of impulsive spending, or will you embrace the path of mindful stewardship?

Your answer to this will determine the your mindset towards reading this literally work.

In the chapters that follow, we will delve deep into the intricacies of saving money the right way, exploring everything from budgeting basics to advanced investment strategies. Along the way, you'll discover practical tips, real-life anecdotes, and actionable insights designed to empower you to take control of your financial future.

But remember, dear reader, true wealth is not merely measured in monetary terms. *It lies in the freedom to live life on your own terms*, to pursue your passions with purpose, and to leave a lasting legacy for generations to come.

So, are you ready to embark on this transformative journey? Are you ready to unlock the secrets of financial success and embrace a future filled with promise and possibility? If so, then turn the page, dear reader, and let the adventure begin.

Title: "The Money Mastery: Unlocking the Secrets of Financial Abundance"

Foreword:

In today's fast-paced and ever-changing world, financial literacy has become more important than ever. Yet, many individuals find themselves navigating the complexities of personal finance without the necessary knowledge and skills to make informed decisions about their money. In this dynamic landscape, a resource like the "The Money Mastery" is invaluable.

As the world of personal finance continues to evolve, it's crucial for individuals to have access to comprehensive, practical, and easy-to-understand guidance to help them navigate their financial journey with confidence and resilience. The "The Money Mastery" fills this need by providing readers with a roadmap to financial success, covering everything from budgeting and saving to investing and planning for the future.

Written by experts in the field of personal finance, this guide offers readers practical advice, actionable strategies, and insightful tips to help them build a solid financial foundation, make smart financial decisions, and achieve their long-term goals. Whether you're a beginner just starting out on your financial journey or an experienced investor looking to refine your strategies, this book has something to offer for everyone.

But perhaps most importantly, the "The Money Mastery" emphasizes the value of lifelong learning and empowerment. By empowering readers with the knowledge, skills, and mindset needed to take control of their finances, this guide not only helps individuals achieve financial independence and security but also fosters a culture of financial literacy and empowerment that benefits society as a whole.

As you embark on this journey through the "The Money Mastery" I encourage you to approach it with an open mind and a willingness to learn. Whether you're seeking practical advice, inspiration, or a fresh perspective on personal finance, you'll find it within these pages. So dive in, explore, and discover the wealth of wisdom that awaits you.

Here's to your financial success and empowerment!

[Kenneth Christopher]

Dedication:

This book is dedicated to all those who aspire to achieve financial independence, security, and freedom.

To the dreamers who envision a brighter financial future and are willing to take action to make it a reality.

To the learners who embrace knowledge and seek to continuously improve their understanding of personal finance.

To the savers who prioritize their financial goals and make prudent decisions to build wealth over time.

To the investors who understand the power of compound interest and harness the potential of the financial markets to grow their assets.

To the planners who carefully strategize and prepare for the challenges and opportunities that lie ahead.

To the resilient who persevere in the face of setbacks, setbacks, and obstacles, knowing that every challenge is an opportunity for growth.

To the mentors who generously share their knowledge, experience, and wisdom to empower others on their financial journey.

And to all those who believe in the transformative power of financial literacy and empowerment to create a more prosperous and equitable world.

May this book serve as a guide, inspiration, and catalyst for your journey to financial success and fulfillment. May you always have the courage to pursue your dreams, the wisdom to make sound financial decisions, and the resilience to overcome any obstacles that stand in your way.

Here's to your financial empowerment and prosperity!

[Kenneth Christopher]

THE MONEY MASTERY

Chapter 1: Understanding Your Financial Landscape

In the vast and ever-changing world of personal finance, the first step towards financial empowerment begins with a clear understanding of your current financial landscape. Just as a skilled navigator must assess the terrain before embarking on a journey, so too must we take stock of our financial situation before charting a course towards our goals.

Assessing Your Current Financial Situation:
Imagine your financial situation as a map, with various landmarks representing your income, expenses, assets, and liabilities. To navigate this terrain effectively, you must first create a detailed inventory of these financial resources.

Start by compiling a list of all your income sources, including your salary, bonuses, freelance earnings, and any other sources of revenue. Next, tally up your expenses, categorizing them into fixed expenses (such as rent or mortgage payments, utilities, and insurance) and variable expenses (such as groceries, dining out, entertainment, and discretionary spending). This exercise will give you a clear picture of your monthly cash flow and help identify areas where you may be overspending.

Once you have a handle on your income and expenses, it's time to take stock of your assets and liabilities. Assets include everything you own that has value, such as savings accounts, investments, real estate, vehicles, and personal belongings. Liabilities, on the other hand, represent your debts and financial obligations, such as credit card balances, student loans, mortgages, and car loans.

By conducting a thorough assessment of your financial situation, you'll gain valuable insights into your overall financial health. You'll be able to see where your money is coming from, where it's going, and how your assets and liabilities stack up. Armed with this information, you'll be better equipped to make informed decisions about how to manage your finances effectively.

Setting Clear Financial Goals:
With a clear understanding of your current financial situation, the next step is to define your financial goals. What do you hope to achieve with your money? Whether it's saving for a down payment on a house, funding your children's education, or building a nest egg for retirement, setting clear and achievable goals is essential for financial success.

When setting your financial goals, remember to make them SMART: Specific, Measurable, Achievable, Relevant, and Time-bound. Instead of saying, "I want to save money," be specific about how much you want to save and by when. For example, "I want to save $10,000 for a down payment on a house within the next two years." This way, you'll have a clear target to aim for and a deadline to keep you accountable.

Identifying Your Spending Habits and Patterns:

Understanding your spending habits and patterns is key to gaining control of your finances. Many of us have unconscious spending habits that can sabotage our financial goals without us even realizing it. By taking the time to track your expenses and identify where your money is going, you can gain valuable insight into your spending behavior and make informed decisions about where to cut back and where to allocate your resources more effectively.

There are many tools and apps available to help you track your spending, from simple budgeting spreadsheets to sophisticated expense tracking software. Choose a method that works for you and commit to tracking your expenses consistently for at least a month. You may be surprised by what you discover!

In this chapter, we've laid the groundwork for understanding your financial landscape. By assessing your current financial situation, setting clear financial goals, and identifying your spending habits and patterns, you'll be well on your way to taking control of your finances and achieving your financial dreams. So, grab your map and compass, dear reader, and let's embark on this journey of financial discovery together.

Assessing your current financial situation is like taking inventory of your financial health. It involves gathering information about your income, expenses, assets, and liabilities to understand where you stand financially. Here's a step-by-step guide to help you assess your financial situation effectively:

1. Compile Your Income Sources: Start by listing all your sources of income, including your salary, wages, bonuses, freelance earnings, rental income, and any other sources of revenue. Make sure to include both regular income and any irregular or sporadic sources.

2. Track Your Expenses: Record all your expenses over a certain period, such as a month. Categorize your expenses into fixed expenses (e.g., rent or mortgage payments, utilities, insurance) and variable expenses (e.g., groceries, dining out, entertainment). This will give you a clear picture of where your money is going and help identify areas where you can potentially cut back.

3. Calculate Your Net Income: Subtract your total expenses from your total income to calculate your net income. This is the amount of money you have left after covering all your expenses. A positive net income indicates that you are living within your means, while a negative net income suggests that you may be overspending and need to make adjustments.

4. Assess Your Assets: List all your assets, including cash, savings accounts, investments (such as stocks, bonds, mutual funds, retirement accounts), real estate properties, vehicles, and any other valuable possessions. Assign a value to each asset based on its current market worth.

5. Calculate Your Liabilities: Next, list all your liabilities, which

include debts and financial obligations such as credit card balances, student loans, mortgages, car loans, personal loans, and any other outstanding debts. Note the total amount owed for each liability.

6. Calculate Your Net Worth: Subtract your total liabilities from your total assets to calculate your net worth. Your net worth represents the difference between what you own (assets) and what you owe (liabilities). It provides a snapshot of your overall financial health and can help you gauge your progress over time.

7. Review Your Financial Goals: Take a moment to review your financial goals and assess whether your current financial situation aligns with your objectives. Are you on track to achieve your goals, or do you need to make adjustments to your spending, saving, or investment strategies?

By assessing your current financial situation thoroughly, you'll gain valuable insights into your financial health and be better equipped to make informed decisions about your money. Remember that financial assessment is not a one-time task; it's an ongoing process that requires regular review and adjustment as your financial circumstances change.

Setting clear financial goals is essential for creating a roadmap to financial success. Here's how you can set SMART financial goals:

1. Specific: Make your goals specific and clearly defined. Instead of saying, "I want to save money," specify how much you want to save and for what purpose. For example, "I want to save $10,000 for a down payment on a house."

2. Measurable: Your goals should be measurable so that you can track your progress and know when you've achieved them. Define concrete metrics to measure your success. For example, "I will save $500 per month towards my down payment."

3. Achievable: Set goals that are challenging yet attainable. Consider your current financial situation, resources, and

capabilities. Avoid setting goals that are too ambitious or unrealistic. Break down larger goals into smaller, manageable steps to make them more achievable.

4. Relevant: Ensure that your goals are relevant to your overall financial objectives and values. They should align with your priorities and aspirations. Ask yourself why each goal is important to you and how it contributes to your financial well-being.

5. Time-bound: Give your goals a deadline or timeframe for completion. This creates a sense of urgency and helps you stay focused and motivated. Set specific dates by which you aim to achieve each goal. For example, "I will save $10,000 for a down payment on a house within the next two years."

Once you've set your SMART financial goals, write them down and review them regularly to stay on track. Break them down into actionable steps and create a plan to achieve them. Monitor your progress periodically and make adjustments as needed. Celebrate your successes along the way and stay committed to achieving your financial goals. Remember that setting clear and achievable goals is the first step towards financial empowerment and a brighter financial future.

Identifying your spending habits and patterns is crucial for gaining control of your finances and making informed decisions about your money. Here's how you can identify and analyze your spending habits effectively:

1. Track Your Expenses: Start by tracking all your expenses over a certain period, such as a month. Keep a record of every penny you spend, whether it's a major purchase or a small daily expense. You can use a budgeting app, spreadsheet, or pen and paper to track

your expenses.

2. Categorize Your Spending: Organize your expenses into categories to see where your money is going. Common categories include housing (rent or mortgage payments), utilities, groceries, transportation, dining out, entertainment, shopping, and miscellaneous expenses. Be thorough and make sure to capture all your spending.

3. Analyze Your Spending Patterns: Once you've tracked your expenses and categorized them, analyze your spending patterns. Look for trends, recurring expenses, and areas where you may be overspending. Are there any patterns or habits that stand out? Do you notice any areas where you could potentially cut back or make changes?

4. Identify Needs vs. Wants: Differentiate between essential expenses (needs) and discretionary spending (wants). Needs are items or services that are necessary for your basic living expenses, such as food, shelter, and utilities. Wants are non-essential items or luxuries that you can live without. Understanding the difference between needs and wants can help you prioritize your spending and make smarter financial decisions.

5. Assess Your Spending Behavior: Reflect on your spending behavior and attitudes towards money. Are you a compulsive shopper who makes impulse purchases? Do you tend to overspend on certain categories, such as dining out or clothing? Understanding your spending behavior can help you identify triggers and develop strategies to curb impulsive spending.

6. Set Spending Limits and Budgets: Once you've identified your spending habits and patterns, set spending limits and budgets for each category. Determine how much you can afford to spend on each expense category based on your income and financial goals. Stick to your budgets as much as possible and avoid overspending.

7. Adjust Your Habits: Use the insights gained from analyzing

your spending habits to make adjustments and changes to your behavior. If you notice that you're spending too much on dining out, for example, try cooking at home more often to save money. Be proactive about finding ways to reduce unnecessary expenses and prioritize your financial goals.

By identifying your spending habits and patterns, you'll gain valuable insights into your financial behavior and be better equipped to make positive changes that will improve your financial well-being. Remember that awareness is the first step towards change, and small adjustments in your spending habits can lead to significant improvements in your financial situation over time.

Chapter 2: Building A Solid Financial Foundation

Building a solid financial foundation is the cornerstone of long-term financial success. In this chapter, we'll explore the essential components of a strong financial foundation and provide actionable steps to help you lay the groundwork for a secure financial future.

Creating a Realistic Budget:
A budget is the foundation of your financial plan, providing a roadmap for how you'll allocate your income to cover expenses, save, and invest. To create a realistic budget, start by listing all your sources of income and categorizing your expenses. Be sure to include both fixed expenses (such as rent or mortgage payments, utilities, and insurance) and variable expenses (such as groceries, transportation, and entertainment). Allocate a portion of your income to savings and investments to ensure that you're building wealth for the future. Review and adjust your budget regularly to reflect changes in your financial situation and priorities.

Emergency Fund Essentials:
An emergency fund is a crucial component of financial stability, providing a safety net to cover unexpected expenses or financial setbacks. Aim to save enough to cover three to six months' worth of living expenses in your emergency fund. Start by setting aside a small portion of your income each month until you reach your target amount. Keep your emergency fund in a separate, easily accessible account, such as a high-yield savings account, so that you can access the funds quickly in case of an emergency.

Debunking Common Money Myths:
In our journey towards financial empowerment, it's essential to separate fact from fiction and debunk common money myths that may be holding us back. Myth #1: "I don't need a budget." Reality: Everyone can benefit from having a budget, regardless of income

level or financial situation. Myth #2: "I'll start saving when I earn more money." Reality: Saving is a habit that should be cultivated regardless of income. Start small and gradually increase your savings over time. Myth #3: "I can't afford to invest." Reality: Investing is essential for building wealth over the long term. You don't need a large sum of money to start investing—there are many low-cost investment options available, such as index funds and robo-advisors.

In this chapter, we've laid the groundwork for building a solid financial foundation. By creating a realistic budget, establishing an emergency fund, and debunking common money myths, you'll be well on your way to achieving financial stability and setting the stage for future financial success. So, roll up your sleeves and let's get started on building the foundation for a brighter financial future.

Creating a realistic budget is the cornerstone of sound financial management. It empowers you to allocate your income effectively, prioritize your spending, and work towards your financial goals. Here's a step-by-step guide to help you create a realistic budget:

1. **Gather Financial Information**: Start by gathering information about your income and expenses. Collect pay stubs, bank statements, and any other relevant documents that detail your financial situation.

2. **Calculate Your Income**: Determine your total monthly income from all sources, including salary, wages, bonuses, freelance work, side hustles, and any other sources of revenue. If your income varies from month to month, calculate an average based on previous months' earnings.

3. **List Your Expenses**: Next, list all your expenses. Categorize your expenses into fixed expenses, such as rent or mortgage

payments, utilities, insurance premiums, and loan payments, and variable expenses, such as groceries, transportation, dining out, entertainment, and discretionary spending.

4. **Track Your Spending**: Review your bank statements and receipts from the past few months to track your spending habits. This will give you a clearer picture of where your money is going and help you identify areas where you may be overspending.

5. **Differentiate Between Needs and Wants**: Differentiate between essential expenses (needs) and discretionary spending (wants). Needs are items or services that are necessary for your basic living expenses, such as food, shelter, and transportation. Wants are non-essential items or luxuries that you can live without. Focus on covering your needs first before allocating funds to wants.

6. **Set Spending Limits**: Once you have a clear understanding of your income and expenses, set spending limits for each category based on your financial priorities and goals. Be realistic about how much you can afford to spend in each category and avoid overspending.

7. **Prioritize Your Financial Goals**: Allocate a portion of your income towards your financial goals, such as saving for emergencies, paying off debt, saving for retirement, or achieving other milestones. Make saving and investing a priority, even if it means cutting back on discretionary spending.

8. **Review and Adjust Regularly**: Review your budget regularly to track your progress and make adjustments as needed. Life circumstances may change, such as changes in income, expenses, or financial goals, so it's important to adapt your budget accordingly.

Remember, creating a realistic budget is not about deprivation or restriction—it's about empowering yourself to make conscious choices about how you use your money to align with your financial goals and priorities. By taking control of your finances through budgeting, you'll be better positioned to achieve financial stability and success in the long run.

Establishing an emergency fund is a critical aspect of financial planning, providing a safety net to cover unexpected expenses and financial setbacks. Here's why it's crucial and how to start building one:

1. **Protection Against Financial Emergencies**: Life is unpredictable, and unexpected expenses can arise at any time, such as medical emergencies, car repairs, home maintenance issues, or sudden job loss. An emergency fund ensures that you have a financial cushion to fall back on when faced with unforeseen circumstances, reducing the need to rely on high-interest credit cards or loans to cover expenses.

2. **Peace of Mind**: Knowing that you have an emergency fund in place can provide peace of mind and alleviate stress during challenging times. It offers a sense of financial security and stability, allowing you to focus on addressing the problem at hand without worrying about how to pay for it.

3. **Prevention of Debt Accumulation**: Without an emergency fund, unexpected expenses can quickly lead to debt accumulation, putting you in a precarious financial situation. By having a dedicated fund set aside for emergencies, you can avoid falling into debt traps and maintain your financial health.

Now, here's how to start building an emergency fund:

1. **Set a Savings Goal**: Determine how much you need to save for your emergency fund. Aim to save enough to cover three to six months' worth of living expenses, including housing, utilities, food, transportation, insurance, and other essential expenses. This amount may vary depending on your individual circumstances, such as your income, expenses, and financial obligations.

2. **Start Small**: If you're unable to save the full amount for your emergency fund right away, start small and gradually work towards your savings goal. Set aside a portion of your income each month specifically for your emergency fund, even if it's just a small amount initially. Consistency is key—automate your savings by setting up automatic transfers from your checking account to your emergency fund account each payday.

3. **Cut Expenses and Increase Income**: Look for ways to reduce discretionary spending and free up extra cash to contribute to your emergency fund. Consider cutting back on non-essential expenses, such as dining out, entertainment, or subscriptions. Additionally, explore opportunities to increase your income through side gigs, freelancing, or selling unused items.

4. **Choose the Right Savings Account**: Keep your emergency fund in a separate, easily accessible account, such as a high-yield savings account or a money market account. These accounts offer liquidity and security while allowing you to earn a competitive interest rate on your savings. Avoid investing your emergency fund in volatile assets or accounts with withdrawal restrictions.

5. **Stay Committed and Consistent**: Building an emergency fund requires discipline and dedication. Stay committed to your savings goal and avoid dipping into your emergency fund for non-essential expenses. Regularly review your budget and make adjustments as needed to ensure that you're making progress towards your savings goal.

By following these steps and prioritizing the establishment of an emergency fund, you'll be better prepared to navigate financial challenges and unexpected expenses with confidence and resilience. Remember that building an emergency fund is a journey, and every dollar saved brings you one step closer to financial security and peace of mind.

Debunking common money myths is essential for making informed financial decisions and achieving financial success. Here are some prevalent money myths and the realities behind them:

Myth #1: "I don't need a budget."
Reality: Budgeting is essential for managing your finances effectively and achieving your financial goals. A budget helps you track your income and expenses, prioritize your spending, and make informed decisions about your money. Without a budget, you may overspend, miss opportunities to save or invest, and struggle to achieve financial stability.

Myth #2: "I'll start saving when I earn more money."
Reality: Saving is a habit that should be cultivated regardless of your income level. Waiting until you earn more money to start saving is a common trap that can lead to financial procrastination and missed opportunities for wealth-building. It's important to prioritize saving, even if it means starting small. Consistency is key—saving a portion of your income regularly, no matter how small, can add up over time and help you achieve your financial goals.

Myth #3: "I can't afford to invest."
Reality: Investing is crucial for building wealth over the long term and achieving financial security. You don't need a large sum of money to start investing—there are many low-cost investment options available, such as index funds, exchange-traded funds (ETFs), and robo-advisors. Additionally, many investment platforms offer fractional shares, allowing you to invest in stocks and other assets with small amounts of money. Start with what you can afford and gradually increase your investments over time as your financial situation improves.

Myth #4: "I'll never get out of debt, so there's no point in trying."
Reality: While getting out of debt may seem daunting, it's entirely possible with dedication, discipline, and a strategic plan. Start by creating a debt repayment plan, prioritizing high-interest debts

first and making extra payments whenever possible. Consider debt consolidation or refinancing options to lower your interest rates and streamline your debt payments. With perseverance and commitment, you can become debt-free and take control of your financial future.

Myth #5: "I need to keep up with the Joneses to be happy."
Reality: Trying to keep up with others' spending habits or lifestyles can lead to financial stress, overspending, and dissatisfaction. True happiness and financial well-being come from living within your means, prioritizing your values and goals, and making intentional choices about how you use your money. Focus on what truly matters to you and your loved ones, and don't be swayed by external pressures or societal expectations.

By debunking these common money myths and embracing the realities behind them, you'll be better equipped to make informed financial decisions, achieve your financial goals, and build a brighter financial future. Remember that financial success is attainable with knowledge, discipline, and perseverance.

Chapter 3: Mastering Mindful Spending

Mindful spending is the art of intentionally directing your money towards the things that truly matter to you, while minimizing wasteful or impulsive spending. In this chapter, we'll explore the principles of mindful spending and provide practical strategies to help you make conscious and deliberate choices about how you use your money.

Differentiating Between Needs and Wants:
At the core of mindful spending is the ability to differentiate between needs and wants. Needs are essential for survival and well-being, such as food, shelter, clothing, and healthcare. Wants, on the other hand, are desires or luxuries that are not strictly necessary for survival. By distinguishing between needs and wants, you can prioritize your spending and allocate your resources more effectively.

Practicing Delayed Gratification Techniques:
Delayed gratification is the practice of resisting the temptation for immediate rewards in favor of long-term benefits. By delaying gratification and exercising patience, you can avoid impulsive purchases and make more thoughtful spending decisions. Practice techniques such as waiting 24 hours before making a non-essential purchase, creating a wishlist for items you want to buy in the future, or setting savings goals to reward yourself for delaying gratification.

Harnessing the Power of Budgeting Apps and Tools:
Budgeting apps and tools can be powerful allies in your quest for mindful spending. These tools help you track your income and expenses, set spending limits, and monitor your progress towards your financial goals. Explore different budgeting apps and tools to find one that suits your needs and preferences. Whether it's a simple budgeting spreadsheet, a dedicated budgeting app, or a

comprehensive financial management platform, find a tool that empowers you to take control of your finances and make informed spending decisions.

Setting Spending Priorities:
Identify your spending priorities by reflecting on your values, goals, and priorities. What matters most to you? What brings you joy and fulfillment? By aligning your spending with your priorities, you can ensure that your money is being used in ways that enhance your quality of life and contribute to your overall well-being. Create a spending plan that reflects your priorities and allocate your resources accordingly, giving more weight to the things that matter most to you.

Practicing Gratitude and Contentment:
Mindful spending is not just about what you buy—it's also about how you perceive and appreciate what you already have. Cultivate gratitude and contentment by focusing on the abundance in your life and appreciating the things you already possess. Practice gratitude exercises such as keeping a gratitude journal, expressing gratitude to others, or simply taking a moment to pause and appreciate the present moment. By cultivating gratitude and contentment, you can reduce the impulse to seek fulfillment through material possessions and find greater satisfaction in life's simple pleasures.

In this chapter, we've explored the principles of mindful spending and provided practical strategies to help you master the art of conscious and deliberate spending. By differentiating between needs and wants, practicing delayed gratification, harnessing the power of budgeting apps and tools, setting spending priorities, and cultivating gratitude and contentment, you can make informed and intentional choices about how you use your money, leading to greater financial well-being and fulfillment.
Differentiating Between Needs and Wants:

1. **Identify Basic Needs**: Start by identifying your basic

needs, which are essential for survival and well-being. These include necessities such as food, shelter, clothing, transportation, healthcare, and utilities. These are the expenses that you must prioritize and allocate your resources towards first.

2. **Evaluate Wants**: Once you've identified your needs, evaluate your wants—desires or luxuries that are not strictly necessary for survival. Wants can include items such as entertainment, dining out, travel, hobbies, and non-essential purchases. While wants can enhance your quality of life and bring you joy, they should be secondary to meeting your basic needs.

3. **Consider Value vs. Cost**: When evaluating wants, consider the value they provide versus their cost. Ask yourself if the item or experience aligns with your values, goals, and priorities. Will it bring you long-term satisfaction and fulfillment, or is it a fleeting indulgence? By weighing the value of each want against its cost, you can make more informed decisions about how to allocate your resources.

Practicing Delayed Gratification Techniques:

1. **Set Waiting Periods**: Implement waiting periods before making non-essential purchases. For example, wait 24 hours or longer before buying something you want. This gives you time to consider whether the purchase is truly necessary and prevents impulsive spending.

2. **Create Wishlists**: Maintain a wishlist of items you want to buy in the future. Whenever you come across something you desire, add it to your wishlist instead of buying it immediately. Review your wishlist periodically and prioritize the items that are most important to you.

3. **Set Savings Goals**: Tie non-essential purchases to savings goals. For example, if you want to buy a new gadget or take a vacation, set a savings goal and allocate a portion of your income towards it each month. Use the delayed gratification of reaching

your savings goal as motivation to resist impulse purchases.

Harnessing the Power of Budgeting Apps and Tools:

1. **Track Your Spending**: Use budgeting apps and tools to track your income and expenses in real-time. These tools categorize your transactions, provide insights into your spending habits, and help you identify areas where you can cut back or save.

2. **Set Spending Limits**: Establish spending limits for different categories of expenses based on your budget and financial goals. Budgeting apps can alert you when you're approaching or exceeding your spending limits, helping you stay on track and avoid overspending.

3. **Automate Savings**: Many budgeting apps allow you to automate savings by setting up recurring transfers from your checking account to your savings or investment accounts. Automating your savings ensures that you consistently set aside money for your financial goals without having to think about it.

By differentiating between needs and wants, practicing delayed gratification techniques, and harnessing the power of budgeting apps and tools, you can cultivate mindful spending habits and make conscious decisions about how you use your money. These strategies empower you to prioritize your financial goals, avoid impulse purchases, and achieve greater financial well-being in the long run.

Certainly, let's delve deeper into each aspect:

Differentiating Between Needs and Wants:

1. **Identify Basic Needs**: Start by clearly defining what constitutes a basic need for you and your household. These are the fundamental requirements for maintaining a reasonable standard of living and ensuring your health, safety, and well-being. Common examples include housing (rent or mortgage payments), utilities (electricity, water, heating), groceries, transportation (commuting costs, vehicle maintenance), healthcare (insurance

premiums, medical expenses), and clothing.

2. **Evaluate Wants**: Once your basic needs are covered, turn your attention to wants—non-essential items or experiences that enhance your lifestyle or bring you joy but are not necessary for survival. Wants can vary greatly from person to person and may include dining out, entertainment (movies, concerts, streaming services), travel, hobbies, leisure activities, fashion, gadgets, and luxury items. While fulfilling wants can contribute to your overall happiness and satisfaction, it's important to recognize them as discretionary expenses and prioritize them accordingly.

3. **Consider Value vs. Cost**: When evaluating wants, consider the value they provide relative to their cost. Reflect on whether a particular want aligns with your values, goals, and priorities. Will it contribute positively to your life in the long run, or is it a fleeting pleasure? Sometimes, spending more on quality items or experiences that provide long-lasting enjoyment or utility can be a wise investment, whereas frivolous or impulsive purchases may not bring lasting satisfaction. By consciously assessing the value of each want against its cost, you can make more informed decisions about how to allocate your resources.

Practicing Delayed Gratification Techniques:

1. **Set Waiting Periods**: Implement waiting periods before making non-essential purchases. For example, if you come across something you want to buy, wait at least 24 hours—or even longer—before making the purchase. This delay allows you to step back, evaluate whether the item is truly necessary or worth the cost, and avoid impulsive spending.

2. **Create Wishlists**: Keep a running wishlist of items or experiences you desire but are not immediately necessary. Instead of buying them on impulse, add them to your wishlist and revisit it periodically. Prioritize the items based on their importance and your financial goals. Creating a wishlist helps you stay focused on your priorities and avoid spontaneous purchases that may not

align with your long-term objectives.

3. **Set Savings Goals**: Tie non-essential purchases to specific savings goals. For instance, if you want to buy a new electronic gadget or go on a vacation, set a savings goal for that particular item or experience. Determine how much you need to save and create a plan to reach your goal within a set timeframe. By linking your spending desires to concrete savings objectives, you imbue your purchases with purpose and discipline, making it easier to resist impulse buys and prioritize your financial well-being.

Harnessing the Power of Budgeting Apps and Tools:

1. **Track Your Spending**: Utilize budgeting apps and tools to monitor your income and expenses systematically. These digital platforms categorize your transactions automatically, providing you with a clear overview of your spending patterns and habits. By regularly tracking your expenditures, you gain valuable insights into where your money is going and can identify areas where you may need to adjust your spending behavior.

2. **Set Spending Limits**: Establish spending limits for different categories of expenses based on your budget and financial objectives. Budgeting apps allow you to set customizable spending limits for various expense categories, such as dining out, entertainment, groceries, and shopping. By setting realistic spending caps, you ensure that your expenditures align with your financial plan and avoid overspending in discretionary areas.

3. **Automate Savings**: Take advantage of automation features offered by budgeting apps to streamline your savings process. Many apps allow you to set up automatic transfers from your checking account to your savings or investment accounts on a recurring basis. By automating your savings contributions, you ensure consistency and discipline in building your financial reserves, even if you have a busy or hectic schedule. Additionally, automated savings make it easier to adhere to your savings goals and prevent the temptation to spend impulsively.

By incorporating these elaborated strategies into your financial management approach, you cultivate mindful spending habits that empower you to make intentional choices about how you use your money. Through a combination of conscious decision-making, delayed gratification, and leveraging digital tools, you can align your spending with your values, goals, and priorities, ultimately fostering greater financial well-being and fulfillment.

Chapter 4: Maximizing Savings Through Smart Shopping

In this chapter, we'll explore strategies and techniques to help you stretch your dollars further and maximize your savings through smart shopping. Whether you're purchasing everyday essentials or treating yourself to a splurge, being savvy about where and how you shop can lead to significant savings over time.

1. **Comparison Shopping**: Before making a purchase, take the time to compare prices across different retailers or online platforms. Use price-comparison websites and apps to quickly find the best deals on the items you need. Don't forget to consider factors such as shipping costs, return policies, and customer reviews when comparing prices.

2. **Use Coupons and Promo Codes**: Coupons and promo codes are valuable tools for saving money on purchases. Look for coupons in newspapers, magazines, and online coupon websites. Additionally, many retailers offer promo codes for discounts or free shipping on their websites. Always check for available coupons and promo codes before completing your purchase.

3. **Shop Sales and Clearance**: Keep an eye out for sales, promotions, and clearance events to score great deals on your favorite items. Many retailers offer seasonal sales, holiday promotions, and clearance markdowns to clear out inventory and attract customers. Plan your purchases around these sales events to take advantage of discounted prices and maximize your savings.

4. **Join Loyalty Programs**: Many retailers offer loyalty programs that reward customers for their purchases. Sign up for loyalty programs at your favorite stores to earn points, discounts, or exclusive offers. Take advantage of rewards programs that offer cashback, discounts, or other perks based on your shopping

habits.

5. **Buy in Bulk**: Buying items in bulk can lead to significant savings, especially for frequently used household goods and non-perishable items. Consider purchasing items like toilet paper, paper towels, cleaning supplies, and pantry staples in bulk to lower your cost per unit and reduce the frequency of shopping trips.

6. **Consider Generic and Store Brands**: Don't overlook generic or store brands when shopping for groceries and household items. Generic brands often offer comparable quality to name brands at a lower price. Experiment with different brands to find affordable alternatives that meet your needs without sacrificing quality.

7. **Utilize Cashback and Rewards Credit Cards**: Cashback and rewards credit cards allow you to earn rewards or cashback on your purchases. Choose a credit card with rewards that align with your spending habits, such as cashback on groceries, gas, or travel expenses. Use your credit card responsibly and pay off your balance in full each month to avoid accruing interest charges.

8. **Negotiate and Haggle**: Don't be afraid to negotiate prices, especially for big-ticket items or services. Many retailers and service providers are willing to negotiate prices or offer discounts to win your business. Be polite and respectful when negotiating, and be prepared to walk away if you can't reach a mutually beneficial agreement.

By implementing these smart shopping strategies, you can maximize your savings and get the most value out of your purchases. Whether you're buying groceries, clothing, electronics, or household essentials, being mindful of where and how you shop can help you keep more money in your pocket and achieve your financial goals faster.

Certainly! Here are strategies for strategic shopping with coupons, sales, and discounts:

1. **Couponing Techniques**:
   - **Online Coupon Websites**: Explore online coupon websites such as RetailMeNot, Coupons.com, and Honey to find a wide range of digital coupons for various retailers and products.
   - **Store Loyalty Programs**: Sign up for store loyalty programs to receive exclusive coupons and discounts tailored to your shopping habits.
   - **Manufacturer Coupons**: Keep an eye out for manufacturer coupons in newspapers, magazines, and online. These coupons can often be combined with store sales for even greater savings.
   - **Stacking Coupons**: Take advantage of opportunities to stack coupons for additional savings. Some stores allow you to use both a manufacturer coupon and a store coupon on the same item, doubling your discount.
   - **Digital Coupons and Apps**: Many retailers offer digital coupons that can be loaded onto loyalty cards or mobile apps for instant savings at checkout. Scan your loyalty card or show the coupon on your smartphone to redeem the discount.

2. **Strategic Sales Shopping**:
   - **Plan Ahead**: Keep track of upcoming sales events, such as Black Friday, Cyber Monday, and seasonal clearance sales. Plan your purchases around these sales to take advantage of discounted prices.
   - **Follow Retailers on Social Media**: Follow your favorite retailers on social media platforms like Facebook, Twitter, and Instagram to stay informed about flash sales, promotions, and exclusive deals.
   - **Shop Off-Season**: Take advantage of end-of-season sales to score discounts on items like clothing, outdoor gear, and holiday decorations. Shopping off-season can save you money while still allowing you to purchase quality products.
   - **Wait for Sales Cycles**: Some items go on sale at predictable times throughout the year. Wait for these sales cycles to purchase items like electronics, appliances, and furniture when prices are

typically lower.

3. **Discount Strategies**:
   - **Student and Military Discounts**: Take advantage of student and military discounts offered by many retailers and service providers. Always ask about available discounts and bring identification to verify your eligibility.
   - **Senior Discounts**: If you're a senior citizen, inquire about senior discounts at participating retailers, restaurants, and entertainment venues. Many businesses offer discounted prices or special promotions for older adults.
   - **Membership Discounts**: Consider joining membership programs like AAA, AARP, or warehouse clubs like Costco and Sam's Club to access exclusive discounts and perks.
   - **Price Matching Policies**: Familiarize yourself with retailers' price matching policies. Some stores will match or beat competitors' prices on identical items, allowing you to get the best deal without shopping around.

By employing these strategies for strategic shopping with coupons, sales, and discounts, you can maximize your savings and get the most value out of your purchases. Whether you're buying groceries, clothing, electronics, or household essentials, being strategic about when and where you shop can help you stretch your budget further and achieve your financial goals more effectively.

Comparison shopping is a powerful strategy for finding the best deals and saving money on your purchases. Here's how to effectively comparison shop:

1. **Research Online**: Start by researching products online to compare prices from different retailers. Use price comparison websites and search engines to quickly find the best deals on the items you're interested in. Pay attention to factors such as shipping costs, return policies, and customer reviews when comparing prices.

2. **Check Multiple Retailers**: Don't settle for the first price you see—check prices from multiple retailers to ensure you're getting the best deal. Look beyond well-known retailers and explore smaller online stores and niche websites, which may offer competitive prices or unique discounts.

3. **Consider All Costs**: When comparing prices, consider all costs associated with the purchase, not just the sticker price. Take into account factors such as shipping fees, taxes, and any additional charges that may apply. A slightly higher upfront cost may be offset by lower shipping fees or better return policies from another retailer.

4. **Use Price Match Guarantees**: Take advantage of price match guarantees offered by many retailers. If you find a lower price for the same item at another store, some retailers will match or beat that price. Be sure to read the retailer's price match policy and follow the instructions for submitting a price match request.

5. **Look for Discounts and Promotions**: Keep an eye out for discounts, promotions, and special offers that can help you save even more on your purchases. Many retailers offer discounts for new customers, seasonal sales, holiday promotions, and clearance markdowns. Sign up for newsletters or follow retailers on social media to stay informed about upcoming sales and exclusive deals.

6. **Consider Additional Benefits**: In addition to price, consider other factors that may influence your purchasing decision, such as product reviews, warranty coverage, customer service, and return policies. A slightly higher price from a reputable retailer with excellent customer service and a generous return policy may be worth it in the long run.

7. **Time Your Purchases**: Timing can play a significant role in finding the best deals. Some retailers offer discounts and promotions during specific times of the year, such as back-to-school sales, Black Friday, Cyber Monday, and end-of-season

clearance events. Plan your purchases around these sales to maximize your savings.

8. **Be Flexible**: Be flexible with your shopping preferences and willing to consider alternative brands or models to find the best deals. Keep an open mind and weigh the pros and cons of different options based on price, quality, and features.

By following these tips for comparison shopping, you can make informed decisions about your purchases and ensure that you're getting the best value for your money. Whether you're buying electronics, clothing, household goods, or gifts, taking the time to compare prices and explore your options can lead to significant savings over time.

Avoiding impulse purchases and buyer's remorse requires mindfulness and self-discipline. Here are some strategies to help you resist the temptation of impulse buying and make more deliberate purchasing decisions:

1. **Create a Shopping List**: Before you go shopping, make a list of the items you need to purchase. Stick to your list and avoid deviating from it, unless you encounter a genuinely necessary item that you forgot to include. Having a shopping list helps you stay focused and reduces the likelihood of impulse purchases.

2. **Set a Budget**: Establish a budget for each shopping trip and adhere to it strictly. Determine how much you can afford to spend on discretionary items, and allocate your budget accordingly. Avoid exceeding your budget by planning your purchases carefully and prioritizing your needs over wants.

3. **Wait Before Buying**: Implement a waiting period before making non-essential purchases. When you feel the urge to buy something on impulse, give yourself time to pause and reconsider. Wait at least 24 hours—or longer, if possible—before making the purchase. Often, the initial impulse will subside, and you'll realize that you don't actually need or want the item as much as you thought.

4. **Evaluate Your Motivations**: Before making a purchase, ask yourself why you want or need the item. Are you buying it out of genuine necessity, or are you seeking temporary gratification or emotional comfort? Be honest with yourself about your motivations and consider whether the purchase aligns with your long-term goals and values.

5. **Identify Triggers**: Pay attention to the factors that trigger impulse buying tendencies, such as boredom, stress, or social influence. Be mindful of situations where you're more susceptible to impulse purchases, such as shopping malls, online sales, or peer pressure. Take proactive steps to minimize exposure to these triggers and develop healthier coping mechanisms for managing stress or boredom.

6. **Practice Mindfulness**: Practice mindfulness and present-moment awareness when shopping. Before making a purchase, take a moment to pause and check in with yourself. Ask yourself if the item is truly necessary, if it aligns with your values and goals, and if you can afford it within your budget. Mindful shopping helps you make more conscious and intentional decisions about your purchases.

7. **Consider the Consequences**: Think about the potential consequences of making an impulse purchase, both in the short term and the long term. Consider the financial impact, the clutter it may create in your home, and whether the item will truly bring you lasting satisfaction and utility. Reflecting on the consequences can help you make a more informed decision and avoid buyer's remorse.

8. **Practice Gratitude**: Cultivate gratitude for what you already have and resist the urge to seek fulfillment through material possessions. Take time to appreciate the things you already own and the experiences you've enjoyed. Practicing gratitude can help shift your focus away from consumerism and towards more meaningful sources of happiness and fulfillment.

By implementing these strategies and cultivating mindful shopping habits, you can avoid impulse purchases and reduce the likelihood of experiencing buyer's remorse. By being intentional about your spending and focusing on what truly matters to you, you can make purchases that align with your values, goals, and priorities, leading to greater satisfaction and financial well-being in the long run.

Avoiding impulse purchases and buyer's remorse is essential for maintaining financial stability and peace of mind. Here are some effective strategies to help you resist the temptation of impulse buying and minimize the risk of regret:

1. **Create a Cooling-Off Period**: Implement a cooling-off period before making any non-essential purchases. When you feel the urge to buy something on impulse, give yourself a set amount of time to reconsider, such as 24 hours or a week. Use this time to evaluate whether the purchase is truly necessary and aligns with your financial goals and priorities.

2. **Stick to a Shopping List**: Before going shopping, make a list of the items you need to purchase and stick to it. Avoid browsing aisles or websites aimlessly, as this increases the likelihood of impulse buying. Having a shopping list helps you stay focused and disciplined, preventing you from succumbing to unplanned purchases.

3. **Set Spending Limits**: Establish spending limits for discretionary purchases and adhere to them rigorously. Determine how much you can afford to spend on non-essential items each month and allocate your budget accordingly. Tracking your spending and staying within your limits helps prevent impulse purchases and ensures that you're making mindful spending decisions.

4. **Identify Triggers**: Pay attention to the factors or situations that trigger impulse buying tendencies, such as stress, boredom, or social influence. Once you identify your triggers, develop

strategies to avoid or mitigate them. For example, if you tend to shop impulsively when stressed, find alternative ways to cope with stress, such as exercising or practicing mindfulness.

5. **Practice Delayed Gratification**: Cultivate the habit of delaying gratification when it comes to purchases. Instead of buying something on impulse, challenge yourself to wait a certain amount of time before making the purchase. Use this time to consider whether the item is truly worth the money and whether you'll still want it after the initial excitement wears off.

6. **Consider the Opportunity Cost**: Before making a purchase, consider the opportunity cost of spending your money on that item. Ask yourself whether there are more meaningful or higher-priority uses for your money, such as saving for emergencies, paying off debt, or investing in your future. By weighing the opportunity cost, you can make more informed decisions about your purchases.

7. **Practice Mindful Spending**: Practice mindfulness and self-awareness when it comes to your spending habits. Before making a purchase, pause and ask yourself why you're buying the item and whether it aligns with your values and goals. By becoming more mindful of your spending choices, you can avoid impulse purchases and make purchases that truly enhance your life.

8. **Reflect on Past Purchases**: Take time to reflect on past impulse purchases and any feelings of regret or dissatisfaction they may have caused. Use these experiences as learning opportunities to inform your future spending decisions. Ask yourself what you could have done differently and how you can avoid similar mistakes in the future.

By implementing these strategies and being intentional about your spending habits, you can avoid impulse purchases and minimize the risk of buyer's remorse. By making mindful and deliberate spending decisions, you can enhance your financial well-being and achieve greater satisfaction and fulfillment in the

KENNETHCHRISTOPHER

long run.

Chapter 5: Supercharging Your Savings With Frugal Living

In this chapter, we'll explore the principles of frugal living and how you can apply them to maximize your savings and achieve your financial goals. Frugal living is about being mindful of your spending, making intentional choices to minimize waste, and prioritizing long-term financial stability over short-term indulgence. Here are some strategies for supercharging your savings through frugal living:

1. **Embrace Minimalism**: Adopting a minimalist lifestyle can help you live more simply and intentionally, focusing on what truly matters to you while reducing unnecessary consumption. Evaluate your possessions and prioritize quality over quantity. Declutter your home and sell or donate items that you no longer need or use. By simplifying your life and living with less, you can save money on purchases, reduce clutter, and cultivate a greater sense of contentment.

2. **Practice Conscious Consumption**: Be mindful of your consumption habits and make deliberate choices about how you spend your money. Before making a purchase, ask yourself whether the item is truly necessary and whether it aligns with your values and goals. Consider the environmental and social impact of your purchases and opt for sustainable, ethically produced products whenever possible. By practicing conscious consumption, you can reduce impulse buying, minimize waste, and save money in the process.

3. **Cook at Home**: Eating out at restaurants or ordering takeout can quickly drain your wallet. Instead, prioritize cooking at home and preparing meals from scratch. Not only is cooking at home more cost-effective, but it also allows you to control the ingredients and portion sizes of your meals. Plan your meals in

advance, shop for groceries strategically, and batch cook or meal prep to save time and money throughout the week.

4. **Reduce Utility Costs**: Take steps to reduce your utility costs and conserve energy in your home. Turn off lights and appliances when not in use, unplug electronics to eliminate phantom power consumption, and adjust your thermostat to save on heating and cooling costs. Consider investing in energy-efficient appliances, LED light bulbs, and smart home devices to further reduce your energy usage and lower your utility bills.

5. **Shop Secondhand**: Embrace the thrift store and secondhand market to find quality items at a fraction of the cost of new. Whether you're shopping for clothing, furniture, electronics, or household goods, secondhand stores, garage sales, and online marketplaces offer a wealth of gently used items at discounted prices. By shopping secondhand, you can save money, reduce waste, and discover unique treasures in the process.

6. **DIY and Repurpose**: Explore do-it-yourself (DIY) projects and repurposing ideas to save money on home improvements, repairs, and personal projects. Whether it's refurbishing furniture, sewing your own clothes, or tackling home maintenance tasks, DIY projects can help you save on labor costs and express your creativity. Look for tutorials and resources online to learn new skills and take on projects that align with your interests and abilities.

7. **Negotiate and Barter**: Don't be afraid to negotiate prices or barter for goods and services. Many retailers, service providers, and individuals are willing to negotiate prices or offer discounts, especially for larger purchases or repeat business. Likewise, consider offering your skills, talents, or unused items in exchange for goods or services you need. By negotiating and bartering, you can stretch your budget further and save money on purchases.

8. **Prioritize Free and Low-Cost Activities**: Look for free or low-cost alternatives to expensive entertainment and leisure

activities. Explore local parks, museums, and community events for opportunities to enjoy enriching experiences without spending a lot of money. Take advantage of libraries, community centers, and online resources for books, movies, and educational materials. By prioritizing free and low-cost activities, you can enjoy life's pleasures while staying within your budget.

By embracing frugal living principles and incorporating these strategies into your daily life, you can supercharge your savings, reduce financial stress, and achieve greater financial freedom. Whether you're saving for a major goal, building an emergency fund, or aiming for early retirement, frugal living can help you make the most of your resources and create a more secure and fulfilling future.

Embracing minimalism involves simplifying your lifestyle by focusing on what truly matters to you and eliminating excess clutter, both physical and mental. Here's how you can simplify your lifestyle and embrace minimalism:

1. **Declutter Your Space**: Start by decluttering your living space and getting rid of items that you no longer need or use. Be ruthless in your decluttering process and ask yourself whether each item brings value or joy to your life. Donate, sell, or recycle items that no longer serve a purpose, and aim to create a clean, clutter-free environment that promotes calmness and clarity.

2. **Prioritize Quality Over Quantity**: Instead of accumulating possessions for the sake of having more, prioritize quality over quantity. Invest in well-made, durable items that will stand the test of time and bring you long-term satisfaction. Choose items that serve multiple purposes or have versatile functionality, reducing the need for excess belongings.

3. **Mindful Consumption**: Practice mindful consumption by being intentional about what you bring into your life. Before making a purchase, ask yourself whether the item is truly necessary and whether it aligns with your values and priorities.

Avoid impulse buying and instead focus on acquiring items that enhance your life and bring genuine value.

4. **Streamline Your Wardrobe**: Simplify your wardrobe by curating a capsule wardrobe consisting of versatile, timeless pieces that can be mixed and matched effortlessly. Keep only clothing items that fit well, flatter your body, and align with your personal style. Donate or sell clothing that no longer fits or suits your lifestyle, and resist the urge to buy new clothing unless it fills a specific gap in your wardrobe.

5. **Digital Decluttering**: Extend your decluttering efforts to your digital life by organizing and streamlining your digital files, emails, and online accounts. Delete unnecessary files and emails, unsubscribe from mailing lists and notifications, and organize your digital documents and photos in a logical, easy-to-access manner. Minimizing digital clutter can help reduce mental overwhelm and improve productivity.

6. **Simplify Your Schedule**: Simplify your schedule by prioritizing activities and commitments that align with your values and goals. Learn to say no to unnecessary obligations and activities that drain your time and energy, and focus on activities that bring you joy and fulfillment. Simplifying your schedule allows you to create more space for rest, relaxation, and meaningful experiences.

7. **Practice Gratitude**: Cultivate gratitude for the things you already have and appreciate the abundance in your life. Shift your focus away from material possessions and toward experiences, relationships, and personal growth. Take time each day to reflect on the things you're grateful for, whether it's the love of family and friends, the beauty of nature, or the simple pleasures of everyday life.

By simplifying your lifestyle and embracing minimalism, you can create a more intentional, meaningful life focused on what truly matters to you. Minimalism is not about deprivation or austerity but about finding joy and contentment in simplicity, mindfulness, and the pursuit of what brings genuine fulfillment.

DIY, or "do it yourself," is a fantastic way to save money by tackling tasks and projects on your own instead of hiring professionals or buying pre-made products. Here's how you can save money by embracing the DIY approach:

1. **Home Repairs and Maintenance**: Instead of hiring contractors for minor repairs or maintenance tasks around your home, learn how to do them yourself. Whether it's fixing a leaky faucet, patching drywall, or unclogging a drain, there are countless resources available online, including tutorials, videos, and DIY forums, that can guide you through the process step by step. By handling these tasks yourself, you can save on labor costs and avoid unnecessary expenses.

2. **Upcycling and Repurposing**: Get creative with upcycling and repurposing items to give them new life and save money on purchasing new goods. Whether it's turning old furniture into stylish decor pieces, repurposing jars and containers for storage, or transforming clothing into trendy accessories, there are endless possibilities for repurposing items that would otherwise end up in the trash. Not only does upcycling save money, but it also reduces waste and promotes sustainability.

3. **DIY Home Decor and Improvements**: Instead of buying expensive home decor items or hiring decorators, consider DIY projects to beautify and improve your living space. From painting walls and refinishing furniture to sewing curtains and crafting wall art, there are countless DIY home decor projects that can enhance your space without breaking the bank. Get inspired by online tutorials, Pinterest boards, and home improvement blogs, and unleash your creativity to personalize your home on a budget.

4. **Meal Preparation and Cooking**: Save money on dining out and pre-packaged convenience foods by preparing meals at home. Cooking your meals from scratch allows you to control the

ingredients, portion sizes, and flavors, while also saving money on restaurant markup and delivery fees. Plan your meals in advance, make use of leftovers, and experiment with budget-friendly recipes to stretch your food budget further.

5. **DIY Gifts and Crafts**: Instead of buying expensive gifts for special occasions, consider making personalized DIY gifts and crafts for your loved ones. Whether it's handmade candles, knitted scarves, or custom photo albums, homemade gifts show thoughtfulness and creativity while also saving money on store-bought presents. Tap into your artistic talents and hobbies to create meaningful gifts that will be cherished for years to come.

6. **Gardening and Landscaping**: Save money on groceries and enhance your outdoor space by growing your fruits, vegetables, and herbs in a garden. Whether you have a backyard, balcony, or windowsill, there are gardening options for every space and skill level. Grow your favorite produce from seeds or seedlings, and enjoy the satisfaction of harvesting fresh, homegrown food while saving money on grocery bills.

7. **DIY Clothing and Fashion**: Instead of splurging on expensive clothing and accessories, consider DIY projects to refresh your wardrobe and express your personal style. Whether it's sewing your own clothing, customizing thrifted finds, or embellishing garments with embroidery or appliqué, DIY fashion allows you to create unique, one-of-a-kind pieces that reflect your individuality while saving money on retail prices.

By embracing the DIY approach and taking on tasks and projects yourself, you can save money, unleash your creativity, and develop valuable skills in the process. Whether it's home repairs, crafting, cooking, or gardening, there are endless opportunities to save money and express yourself through hands-on, do-it-yourself projects.

Repurposing and upcycling are fantastic ways to find value in everyday items, reduce waste, and save money. Here are some creative ideas for repurposing and upcycling common household items:

1. **Glass Jars and Bottles**: Instead of tossing glass jars and bottles into the recycling bin, repurpose them for various purposes around your home. Use glass jars to store bulk foods, spices, or homemade jams and sauces. Turn empty wine bottles into stylish vases or candle holders by removing the labels and adding decorative touches. You can also create homemade salad dressings or infused oils in repurposed glass bottles.

2. **Corks**: Save wine corks and repurpose them into useful household items. Glue multiple corks together to create a trivet for hot pots and pans in the kitchen. Slice corks into thin discs and use them as drawer dividers or to cushion furniture legs and prevent scratches on floors. Corks can also be transformed into coasters, keychains, or even DIY stamps for crafting projects.

3. **Old Furniture**: Give old furniture new life by upcycling it into something fresh and functional. Sand and repaint a worn-out dresser or side table to match your decor and breathe new life into the piece. Convert an old door or window frame into a unique headboard for your bed. Use salvaged wood to build shelves, benches, or planters for your home or garden. With a little creativity and elbow grease, you can transform old furniture into stylish and practical pieces that add character to your space.

4. **Fabric Scraps**: Instead of throwing away fabric scraps, repurpose them into small sewing projects or crafts. Turn fabric scraps into patchwork quilts, pillow covers, or fabric coasters. Use scraps of denim to make stylish tote bags or upcycled jeans into trendy denim shorts or skirts. Fabric scraps can also be repurposed into fabric gift wrap, reusable produce bags, or even handmade dolls or stuffed animals for children.

5. **Plastic Containers**: Repurpose plastic containers and bottles for storage and organization purposes. Use empty yogurt containers or plastic bins to organize craft supplies, office

supplies, or small hardware items like nails and screws. Cut off the tops of plastic bottles and use them as planters for small herbs or succulents. Repurposed plastic containers can also be used as makeshift plant saucers, paint palettes, or seedling starters in the garden.

6. **Newspapers and Magazines**: Instead of tossing old newspapers and magazines into the recycling bin, repurpose them for various projects. Use newspaper to create biodegradable seedling pots for starting plants indoors. Roll up magazine pages and glue them together to make colorful beads for jewelry or decorative accents. Newspapers can also be used as packing material for shipping fragile items or as a natural weed barrier in the garden.

7. **Tin Cans**: Repurpose tin cans into versatile storage containers or decorative accents for your home. Remove the labels from tin cans and use them to store kitchen utensils, office supplies, or small bathroom items like cotton swabs or toothbrushes. Paint or decorate tin cans with fabric, paper, or ribbon to create stylish pencil holders, flower vases, or candle holders. Tin cans can also be punched with holes and turned into luminaries for outdoor lighting.

By repurposing and upcycling everyday items, you can find value in what might otherwise be considered waste and save money in the process. Get creative, think outside the box, and discover the endless possibilities for repurposing and upcycling common household items in your home.

Chapter 6: Investing In Your Future

In this chapter, we'll delve into the importance of investing in your future and explore various strategies for building wealth, achieving financial security, and reaching your long-term goals. Investing isn't just about putting money into stocks or bonds—it's about making smart decisions today that will pay off in the future and provide you with the resources you need to live a fulfilling life. Here are some key principles and strategies for investing in your future:

1. **Setting Financial Goals**: Start by defining your financial goals and aspirations. Whether it's saving for retirement, buying a home, funding your children's education, or traveling the world, having clear goals will guide your investment strategy and help you stay focused on what's truly important to you.

2. **Building an Emergency Fund**: Before diving into long-term investments, ensure you have a solid financial foundation by building an emergency fund. Aim to save three to six months' worth of living expenses in a readily accessible account to cover unexpected expenses or financial setbacks. An emergency fund provides a safety net and peace of mind, allowing you to weather financial storms without derailing your long-term plans.

3. **Diversifying Your Portfolio**: Diversification is key to managing risk and maximizing returns in your investment portfolio. Spread your investments across a mix of asset classes, such as stocks, bonds, real estate, and alternative investments, to reduce exposure to any single market or sector. Diversification helps smooth out fluctuations in your portfolio's value and can enhance long-term performance.

4. **Investing in Retirement Accounts**: Take advantage of tax-advantaged retirement accounts such as 401(k)s, IRAs, and Roth IRAs to save for retirement. Contribute regularly to these accounts

and take advantage of any employer matching contributions offered through workplace retirement plans. Maximize your contributions each year to take full advantage of tax benefits and accelerate your retirement savings.

5. **Consistent Saving and Investing**: Make saving and investing a habit by automating contributions to your investment accounts. Set up automatic transfers from your paycheck or bank account to your retirement accounts and investment accounts. Consistent saving and investing over time allow you to benefit from compound interest and dollar-cost averaging, helping your investments grow steadily over the long term.

6. **Educating Yourself**: Take the time to educate yourself about investing and financial planning. Read books, attend seminars, and seek advice from reputable financial professionals to improve your knowledge and confidence in managing your finances. Understanding basic investment principles and staying informed about market trends and economic indicators will empower you to make informed decisions about your investments.

7. **Managing Risk**: Understand and manage the risks associated with investing. While investing inevitably involves some level of risk, you can mitigate risk through diversification, asset allocation, and periodic portfolio rebalancing. Avoid making impulsive decisions based on short-term market fluctuations, and maintain a long-term perspective when evaluating your investment strategy.

8. **Seeking Professional Advice**: Consider working with a qualified financial advisor or investment professional to develop a personalized investment plan tailored to your goals, risk tolerance, and time horizon. A financial advisor can provide valuable guidance, objective analysis, and strategic recommendations to help you make informed decisions and navigate complex financial markets.

Investing in your future is about more than just accumulating wealth—it's about securing your financial well-being, achieving your dreams, and enjoying a comfortable and fulfilling lifestyle in the years to come. By setting clear goals, diversifying your investments, and staying disciplined in your saving and investing habits, you can build a solid foundation for a brighter financial future. Remember that investing is a journey, not a destination, and that patience, persistence, and prudent decision-making are key to long-term success.

Exploring Different Investment Options: Stocks, Bonds, Real Estate, and More

When building an investment portfolio, it's essential to diversify across different asset classes to spread risk and maximize returns. Here are some popular investment options to consider:

1. **Stocks**: Stocks represent ownership in publicly traded companies and offer the potential for high returns over the long term. Investing in individual stocks allows you to participate in the growth and profitability of specific companies. However, stocks can be volatile, and individual companies can face risks such as market downturns, competition, and management changes.

2. **Bonds**: Bonds are debt securities issued by governments, municipalities, or corporations to raise capital. When you invest in bonds, you're essentially lending money to the issuer in exchange for periodic interest payments and the return of the principal amount at maturity. Bonds are generally considered less risky than stocks but offer lower potential returns. They can provide stability and income to a diversified investment portfolio.

3. **Real Estate**: Real estate investments can take various forms, including residential properties, commercial properties, and real estate investment trusts (REITs). Real estate offers the potential for appreciation in property values, rental income, and tax benefits such as depreciation deductions. However, real estate investments can be illiquid, require significant upfront capital,

and involve ongoing management responsibilities.

4. **Mutual Funds and Exchange-Traded Funds (ETFs)**: Mutual funds and ETFs pool money from multiple investors to invest in a diversified portfolio of stocks, bonds, or other assets. Mutual funds are actively managed by professional fund managers who aim to outperform the market, while ETFs typically track a specific index or sector. Mutual funds and ETFs offer diversification, liquidity, and convenience for investors seeking exposure to a broad range of asset classes.

5. **Alternative Investments**: Alternative investments include assets such as hedge funds, private equity, commodities, and cryptocurrencies. These investments typically have low correlations with traditional asset classes like stocks and bonds, offering potential diversification benefits. However, alternative investments can be complex, illiquid, and speculative, requiring careful consideration and due diligence before investing.

Understanding Risk and Return: Building a Diversified Investment Portfolio

When constructing a diversified investment portfolio, it's essential to consider the trade-off between risk and return. Here are some key principles to keep in mind:

1. **Risk Tolerance**: Assess your risk tolerance, or your ability and willingness to tolerate fluctuations in the value of your investments. Generally, younger investors with a longer time horizon can afford to take on more risk, as they have more time to recover from market downturns. Older investors or those nearing retirement may prefer a more conservative investment approach to preserve capital.

2. **Asset Allocation**: Determine the appropriate asset allocation for your investment portfolio based on your risk tolerance, financial goals, and time horizon. Asset allocation involves dividing your investments across different asset classes such as

stocks, bonds, and real estate to achieve a balance between risk and return. A well-diversified portfolio can help mitigate risk and optimize returns over time.

3. **Correlation**: Consider the correlation between different asset classes when constructing your investment portfolio. Correlation measures the degree to which the returns of one asset move in relation to another. By investing in assets with low or negative correlations, you can reduce the overall volatility of your portfolio and enhance diversification.

4. **Rebalancing**: Regularly review and rebalance your investment portfolio to maintain your target asset allocation and risk profile. Rebalancing involves buying and selling assets to bring your portfolio back into alignment with your desired allocation. Rebalancing ensures that you're not overly exposed to any single asset class and helps you stay on track to achieve your long-term investment goals.

Starting Small: How to Begin Investing with Limited Funds

You don't need a large sum of money to start investing—there are several ways to begin investing with limited funds:

1. **Start with a Retirement Account**: Contribute to a tax-advantaged retirement account such as a 401(k), IRA, or Roth IRA. Many retirement accounts have low minimum investment requirements and offer tax benefits such as tax-deferred growth or tax-free withdrawals in retirement. Take advantage of employer matching contributions in workplace retirement plans to maximize your savings.

2. **Invest in Fractional Shares**: Consider investing in fractional shares of stocks or ETFs through brokerage platforms that offer fractional investing. Fractional investing allows you to purchase a partial share of a stock or ETF, making it more accessible for investors with limited funds. This allows you to diversify your portfolio and invest in high-priced stocks or ETFs with smaller

amounts of money.

3. **Automate Your Investments**: Set up automatic contributions to your investment accounts on a regular basis, such as monthly or biweekly. Automating your investments helps you stay disciplined and consistent with your saving and investing habits, regardless of the amount you're able to invest. Over time, small, regular contributions can add up and grow into a significant investment portfolio.

4. **Consider Robo-Advisors**: Robo-advisors are automated investment platforms that use algorithms to create and manage diversified investment portfolios based on your risk tolerance and financial goals. Many robo-advisors have low minimum investment requirements and offer a range of investment options, making them accessible to investors with limited funds. Robo-advisors provide a hands-off approach to investing, making them suitable for beginner investors.

5. **Educate Yourself**: Take the time to educate yourself about investing and personal finance. There are countless resources available online, including books, articles, podcasts, and educational websites, that can help you learn the basics of investing and develop a solid investment strategy. By empowering yourself with knowledge, you can make informed decisions and navigate the world of investing with confidence, regardless of your initial investment amount.

By exploring different investment options, understanding the relationship between risk and return, and starting small with limited funds, you can begin your investment journey and work towards achieving your long-term financial goals. Remember that investing is a marathon, not a sprint, and that patience, discipline, and consistency are key to success over time.

Chapter 7: Navigating Financial Challenges

Life is full of unexpected twists and turns, and financial challenges can arise when you least expect them. In this chapter, we'll explore common financial challenges that many people face and provide strategies for navigating them effectively. Whether you're dealing with debt, job loss, medical expenses, or other financial setbacks, it's essential to approach these challenges with resilience, resourcefulness, and a proactive mindset. Here are some key topics we'll cover:

1. **Managing Debt**: Debt can be a significant source of financial stress for many individuals and families. Whether it's credit card debt, student loans, or medical bills, managing debt effectively is essential for achieving financial stability. We'll discuss strategies for paying down debt, negotiating with creditors, and avoiding common debt traps.

2. **Coping with Job Loss or Income Reduction**: Losing a job or experiencing a sudden reduction in income can be emotionally and financially challenging. We'll explore strategies for coping with job loss, including assessing your financial situation, creating a budget, exploring alternative income sources, and updating your resume and networking to find new employment opportunities.

3. **Dealing with Medical Expenses**: Unexpected medical expenses can quickly derail your finances and lead to significant debt. We'll discuss strategies for managing medical expenses, such as reviewing your health insurance coverage, negotiating medical bills, setting up payment plans, and exploring government assistance programs or charitable organizations that may provide financial assistance for medical bills.

4. **Building an Emergency Fund**: Having an emergency fund is crucial for weathering financial storms and covering unexpected

expenses. We'll discuss the importance of building an emergency fund, how much you should save, and where to keep your emergency savings. We'll also explore strategies for starting and growing your emergency fund, even if you're on a tight budget.

5. **Protecting Against Financial Risks**: Insurance can provide valuable protection against financial risks such as illness, disability, property damage, and liability. We'll discuss the different types of insurance coverage you may need, including health insurance, disability insurance, life insurance, auto insurance, homeowners or renters insurance, and umbrella liability insurance. We'll also explore ways to lower your insurance premiums without sacrificing coverage.

6. **Planning for Retirement**: Planning for retirement is a long-term financial goal that requires careful consideration and preparation. We'll discuss strategies for saving for retirement, including contributing to employer-sponsored retirement plans like 401(k)s or 403(b)s, opening individual retirement accounts (IRAs), and investing in taxable brokerage accounts. We'll also explore retirement income sources such as Social Security, pensions, annuities, and retirement withdrawals.

7. **Seeking Financial Guidance and Support**: If you're struggling to navigate financial challenges on your own, don't hesitate to seek guidance and support from financial professionals, counselors, or community resources. We'll discuss the importance of reaching out for help when needed and how to find reputable financial professionals who can provide personalized advice and assistance.

8. **Developing Resilience and Mindset**: Finally, we'll discuss the importance of developing resilience and a positive mindset when facing financial challenges. Cultivating resilience involves staying flexible, adapting to change, and learning from setbacks. We'll explore strategies for building resilience, such as maintaining a sense of perspective, focusing on solutions rather than dwelling

on problems, and practicing self-care to manage stress and anxiety.

By addressing financial challenges head-on, staying proactive, and seeking support when needed, you can overcome obstacles, build financial resilience, and work towards achieving your long-term financial goals. Remember that financial challenges are a normal part of life, and with perseverance and determination, you can navigate them successfully and emerge stronger on the other side. Dealing with debt can be daunting, but with the right strategies, you can take control of your finances and work towards becoming debt-free. Here are some effective strategies for debt repayment and avoidance:

1. **Create a Budget**: Start by creating a realistic budget that outlines your monthly income and expenses. Identify areas where you can cut back on discretionary spending and allocate more money towards debt repayment. A budget serves as a roadmap for managing your finances and prioritizing debt payments.

2. **Prioritize High-Interest Debt**: If you have multiple debts, focus on paying off high-interest debt first. High-interest debt, such as credit card debt or payday loans, can quickly spiral out of control due to compounding interest charges. Paying off high-interest debt saves you money on interest payments and accelerates your journey to debt freedom.

3. **Snowball or Avalanche Method**: Choose a debt repayment strategy that works best for you, such as the snowball or avalanche method. With the snowball method, you pay off your debts in order of smallest to largest balance, gaining momentum as you eliminate each debt. With the avalanche method, you prioritize debts based on interest rate, paying off the highest-interest debt first to minimize interest costs over time.

4. **Negotiate with Creditors**: If you're struggling to keep up with debt payments, don't hesitate to contact your creditors and negotiate for more favorable terms. You may be able to negotiate

lower interest rates, reduced monthly payments, or a repayment plan that better fits your financial situation. Many creditors are willing to work with you to find a solution that prevents default and preserves their ability to collect on the debt.

5. **Consolidate or Refinance Debt**: Consider consolidating or refinancing your debt to lower your interest rates and simplify your repayment process. Debt consolidation involves combining multiple debts into a single loan with a lower interest rate, making it easier to manage your payments. Refinancing allows you to replace high-interest debt with a new loan at a lower interest rate, reducing your overall interest costs.

6. **Avoid Taking on New Debt**: While repaying existing debt, avoid taking on new debt that could worsen your financial situation. Be mindful of your spending habits and resist the temptation to use credit cards or take out loans for non-essential purchases. Focus on living within your means and building a solid financial foundation that prioritizes debt repayment and financial stability.

7. **Increase Your Income**: Look for opportunities to increase your income and accelerate debt repayment. Consider taking on a part-time job, freelancing, or starting a side hustle to generate extra income. Use any additional income to make extra payments towards your debts, speeding up your progress and reducing the total interest paid over time.

8. **Seek Professional Help if Needed**: If you're overwhelmed by debt and struggling to make progress on your own, consider seeking professional help from a credit counselor or debt management agency. A credit counselor can help you create a personalized debt repayment plan, negotiate with creditors on your behalf, and provide financial education and support to help you regain control of your finances.

By implementing these strategies and staying committed to your debt repayment goals, you can take control of your finances, eliminate debt, and achieve greater financial freedom. Remember that becoming debt-free takes time and perseverance, but the rewards of financial security and peace of mind are well worth the effort.

Overcoming financial hurdles such as job loss, medical emergencies, and unexpected expenses requires resilience, resourcefulness, and a proactive approach to managing your finances. Here are strategies for navigating these challenges:

1. **Emergency Fund**: Building an emergency fund is essential for weathering financial storms and covering unexpected expenses. Aim to save three to six months' worth of living expenses in a readily accessible account to cushion the blow of job loss, medical emergencies, or other financial setbacks. Having an emergency fund provides a financial safety net and peace of mind, allowing you to cover essential expenses while you navigate difficult times.

2. **Budgeting and Prioritizing Expenses**: Create a budget that prioritizes essential expenses such as housing, food, utilities, and healthcare. Identify areas where you can cut back on discretionary spending and allocate more money towards necessities. Trim unnecessary expenses, negotiate bills, and look for ways to save money on everyday purchases to stretch your budget further during times of financial hardship.

3. **Seeking Alternative Income Sources**: If you experience job loss or a reduction in income, explore alternative income sources to supplement your earnings and cover expenses. Consider taking on temporary work, freelancing, gig economy jobs, or part-time employment to generate income while you search for new job opportunities. Look for creative ways to monetize your skills, hobbies, or assets to generate cash flow during challenging times.

4. **Reviewing Insurance Coverage**: Review your insurance coverage, including health insurance, disability insurance, life insurance, and property insurance, to ensure you're adequately

protected against unexpected events. Understand your policy coverage, deductibles, and out-of-pocket costs, and explore options for adjusting your coverage or shopping around for more affordable insurance options if necessary. Insurance can provide valuable protection against financial risks and help mitigate the impact of unexpected expenses.

5. **Negotiating Payment Plans and Assistance Programs**: If you're facing medical emergencies or unexpected expenses, don't hesitate to reach out to creditors, lenders, or service providers to negotiate payment plans or request assistance. Many creditors are willing to work with you to create a repayment plan that fits your financial situation and prevents default. Explore government assistance programs, charitable organizations, and community resources that may offer financial assistance or support services for individuals facing financial hardship.

6. **Prioritizing Health and Well-being**: During times of financial stress, prioritize your health and well-being to maintain resilience and cope with challenges effectively. Take care of yourself physically, mentally, and emotionally by eating healthily, exercising regularly, getting enough sleep, and seeking support from friends, family, or mental health professionals if needed. Practice stress-reduction techniques such as mindfulness, meditation, or deep breathing to manage anxiety and maintain a positive outlook during difficult times.

7. **Seeking Professional Guidance**: If you're struggling to overcome financial hurdles on your own, don't hesitate to seek professional guidance from financial advisors, counselors, or social workers who can provide personalized advice and assistance. Financial professionals can help you assess your financial situation, explore options for managing debt or expenses, and develop a plan for regaining financial stability. They can also provide valuable support and guidance as you navigate challenging circumstances and work towards achieving your long-term financial goals.

By implementing these strategies and staying proactive in managing your finances, you can overcome financial hurdles such as job loss, medical emergencies, and unexpected expenses, and emerge stronger and more resilient on the other side. Remember that difficult times are temporary, and with perseverance, resourcefulness, and support, you can overcome obstacles and create a brighter financial future for yourself and your loved ones. Seeking professional help from financial advisors can provide valuable guidance and support in navigating complex financial decisions, planning for the future, and achieving your financial goals. Here's when and how to consult financial advisors effectively:

1. **When to Consult Financial Advisors**:

   - **Life Transitions**: Consult a financial advisor during significant life transitions such as marriage, divorce, parenthood, retirement, inheritance, or career changes. A financial advisor can help you navigate these transitions and make informed decisions that align with your financial goals and priorities.

   - **Complex Financial Situations**: If you're facing complex financial situations such as managing multiple assets, planning for estate and legacy, optimizing tax strategies, or navigating business finances, consulting a financial advisor can provide expert guidance and strategic advice tailored to your unique circumstances.

   - **Long-Term Planning**: Whether you're planning for retirement, saving for your children's education, or building wealth for the future, consulting a financial advisor can help you develop a comprehensive financial plan that addresses your long-term goals, risk tolerance, and investment strategy.

   - **Financial Crisis or Hardship**: During times of financial crisis or hardship, such as job loss, medical emergencies, or unexpected expenses, seeking guidance from a financial advisor can help you assess your options, prioritize expenses, and develop a plan to regain financial stability.

2. **How to Consult Financial Advisors**:

   - **Research and Due Diligence**: Research different types of financial advisors, including certified financial planners (CFPs), registered investment advisors (RIAs), and wealth managers, to find a professional who aligns with your needs, values, and goals. Look for advisors with relevant credentials, experience, and a fiduciary duty to act in your best interest.

   - **Initial Consultation**: Schedule an initial consultation with one or more financial advisors to discuss your financial situation, goals, and concerns. Use this opportunity to assess the advisor's expertise, communication style, and approach to financial planning. Ask questions about their qualifications, fees, investment philosophy, and how they will work with you to achieve your objectives.

   - **Define Expectations and Goals**: Clearly define your expectations and goals for working with a financial advisor. Be upfront about your financial situation, risk tolerance, investment preferences, and any specific concerns or priorities you have. Communicate your short-term and long-term objectives so that the advisor can tailor their recommendations accordingly.

   - **Review Recommendations and Proposals**: After the initial consultation, review the advisor's recommendations and proposals carefully. Consider factors such as investment strategies, risk management, fees and expenses, tax implications, and how the proposed plan aligns with your financial goals and values. Ask for clarification or additional information as needed before making a decision.

   - **Ongoing Communication and Review**: Establish a system for ongoing communication and review with your financial advisor to monitor progress, adjust strategies as needed, and stay informed about changes in your financial situation or goals. Regular check-ins and reviews ensure that your financial plan remains aligned with your objectives and adapts to evolving circumstances over time.

3. **Red Flags to Watch Out For**:

   - **Conflicts of Interest**: Be wary of financial advisors who have conflicts of interest or receive commissions or incentives for recommending specific products or services. Look for advisors who operate under a fiduciary standard and are legally obligated to act in your best interest.

   - **High Pressure Sales Tactics**: Avoid advisors who use high-pressure sales tactics or make unrealistic promises about investment returns. A reputable financial advisor should prioritize your needs, goals, and risk tolerance, and provide transparent and realistic recommendations based on sound financial principles.

   - **Lack of Transparency**: Transparency is crucial when working with a financial advisor. Make sure you fully understand the advisor's fees, compensation structure, potential conflicts of interest, and how they are regulated or licensed. If an advisor is evasive or unwilling to provide clear information, consider it a red flag and seek guidance elsewhere.

By consulting financial advisors at the right time, conducting thorough research, defining expectations and goals, and maintaining open communication, you can benefit from expert guidance and support in achieving your financial objectives and navigating complex financial decisions effectively. Remember that finding the right financial advisor is an important step towards building a successful financial future, so take the time to choose wisely and build a trusting relationship based on mutual respect and collaboration.

Chapter 8: Cultivating Long-Term Financial Success

In this chapter, we'll explore strategies for cultivating long-term financial success and building a solid foundation for a secure and prosperous future. Whether you're just starting your financial journey or looking to enhance your existing financial plan, these principles will guide you towards achieving your goals and living a fulfilling life.

1. **Setting Clear Financial Goals**: Begin by defining your financial goals and aspirations. Whether it's saving for retirement, buying a home, starting a business, or traveling the world, having clear and achievable goals provides direction and motivation for your financial journey. Break down your goals into smaller, actionable steps and create a timeline for achieving them.

2. **Living Within Your Means**: Practice living within your means by spending less than you earn and avoiding unnecessary debt. Adopt a frugal mindset and prioritize spending on essentials and experiences that bring value and joy to your life. Avoid lifestyle inflation and resist the temptation to keep up with others' spending habits. Focus on building wealth gradually through disciplined saving, investing, and smart financial decisions.

3. **Creating and Following a Budget**: Develop a budget that aligns with your financial goals and values. Track your income and expenses, categorize spending, and identify areas where you can cut back or reallocate resources. Use budgeting tools and apps to streamline the process and stay organized. Regularly review and adjust your budget as needed to accommodate changes in your financial situation or goals.

4. **Investing for the Future**: Invest wisely for the future by diversifying your investment portfolio, maximizing tax-advantaged accounts, and staying disciplined in your investment

strategy. Consider your risk tolerance, time horizon, and financial goals when selecting investments. Focus on long-term growth and wealth accumulation through a balanced approach to asset allocation and periodic portfolio rebalancing.

5. **Saving and Building Emergency Funds**: Build an emergency fund to cover unexpected expenses and financial setbacks. Aim to save three to six months' worth of living expenses in a readily accessible account to provide a safety net during times of uncertainty. Automate your savings and contributions to retirement accounts to make saving a consistent habit and prioritize building financial resilience.

6. **Managing Debt Effectively**: Manage debt effectively by paying down high-interest debt aggressively and avoiding unnecessary debt accumulation. Use debt strategically for investments that generate positive returns, such as education or home ownership, but avoid excessive debt that hampers your financial freedom. Develop a debt repayment plan and stay focused on becoming debt-free over time.

7. **Continuing Financial Education**: Commit to lifelong learning and continuous improvement in your financial knowledge and skills. Stay informed about personal finance topics, investment strategies, tax laws, and economic trends through books, articles, podcasts, courses, and seminars. Take advantage of educational resources and seek guidance from financial professionals to make informed decisions and adapt to changing circumstances.

8. **Protecting Your Assets and Income**: Safeguard your assets and income against unexpected risks by maintaining adequate insurance coverage, including health insurance, disability insurance, life insurance, and property insurance. Review your insurance policies regularly to ensure they provide adequate protection for your needs and circumstances. Consider additional measures such as estate planning, asset protection strategies, and

legal safeguards to protect your financial well-being and legacy.

9. **Giving Back and Sharing Success**: Cultivate a spirit of generosity and giving back to others as part of your long-term financial success. Support charitable causes and organizations that align with your values and priorities. Share your knowledge, experience, and resources with others to empower them on their own financial journeys. By giving back to your community and making a positive impact in the lives of others, you create a legacy of generosity and compassion that extends beyond financial wealth.

By embracing these principles and integrating them into your financial habits and mindset, you can cultivate long-term financial success and achieve your goals with confidence and purpose. Remember that financial success is not just about accumulating wealth—it's about living a meaningful and fulfilling life, making a positive impact in the world, and enjoying peace of mind and security for yourself and your loved ones. Commit to your financial journey, stay disciplined in your actions, and celebrate the milestones along the way as you create the future you envision.

Setting and reviewing financial milestones is a crucial part of achieving long-term financial success. Here's how to set and review your financial milestones effectively:

1. **Identify Your Financial Goals**: Start by identifying your financial goals, both short-term and long-term. These may include saving for retirement, buying a home, paying off debt, funding your children's education, starting a business, or traveling the world. Write down your goals and prioritize them based on their importance and timeline.

2. **Quantify Your Goals**: Assign specific, measurable targets to each of your financial goals. For example, instead of saying you want to "save for retirement," specify how much you want to save by a certain age or retirement date. Quantifying your goals

makes them more tangible and actionable, helping you track your progress over time.

3. **Set SMART Milestones**: Use the SMART criteria—Specific, Measurable, Achievable, Relevant, and Time-bound—to set your financial milestones. Each milestone should be clearly defined, measurable, realistic, relevant to your overall financial plan, and tied to a specific timeframe. For example, "Pay off $10,000 in credit card debt within two years" is a SMART milestone.

4. **Break Down Larger Goals**: Break down larger, long-term goals into smaller, more manageable milestones. This makes it easier to track progress and stay motivated along the way. For example, if your goal is to save $100,000 for a down payment on a house in five years, set annual or quarterly savings targets to reach that goal incrementally.

5. **Track Your Progress Regularly**: Monitor your progress towards each financial milestone on a regular basis. Use tools such as spreadsheets, budgeting apps, or financial software to track income, expenses, savings, investments, and debt repayment. Review your progress monthly, quarterly, or annually to see how you're tracking towards your goals.

6. **Celebrate Achievements**: Celebrate your achievements and milestones along the way to stay motivated and encouraged. Recognize your progress, whether it's reaching a savings target, paying off a debt, or achieving a financial milestone ahead of schedule. Celebrating small victories boosts morale and reinforces positive financial habits.

7. **Adjust as Needed**: Be flexible and willing to adjust your financial milestones as circumstances change. Life events, economic conditions, and personal priorities may shift over time, requiring you to reassess your goals and adjust your plans accordingly. Regularly review and revise your financial milestones to ensure they remain relevant and achievable.

8. **Seek Professional Guidance**: Consider consulting with a financial advisor or planner to help you set and review your financial milestones. A professional can provide personalized guidance, expertise, and accountability to help you make informed decisions and stay on track towards achieving your goals.

9. **Stay Focused on the Big Picture**: Keep the big picture in mind as you work towards your financial milestones. Remember why you set these goals in the first place and how achieving them will improve your life and financial well-being. Stay focused, stay disciplined, and stay committed to your financial journey, knowing that each milestone brings you one step closer to your ultimate vision of success.

By setting SMART financial milestones, tracking your progress regularly, celebrating achievements, and staying flexible in your approach, you can effectively navigate your financial journey and achieve the goals that matter most to you. Remember that financial success is a journey, not a destination, and that each milestone reached is a testament to your hard work, determination, and commitment to creating a brighter financial future.

Practicing consistency and discipline is key to achieving long-term financial success. Here are some strategies to help you cultivate these essential qualities:

1. **Establish Clear Goals**: Start by defining clear and achievable financial goals. Whether it's saving for retirement, paying off debt, or building an emergency fund, having specific goals provides direction and motivation for your financial journey. Write down your goals, break them down into smaller milestones, and create a timeline for achieving them.

2. **Develop a Routine**: Establish a routine for managing your finances and stick to it consistently. Set aside time each week or month to review your budget, track your expenses, and monitor

your progress towards your goals. Treat your financial tasks with the same level of importance as other commitments in your life to ensure they receive the attention they deserve.

3. **Automate Your Finances**: Take advantage of automation tools and technology to streamline your financial tasks and ensure consistency. Set up automatic transfers to your savings and investment accounts, schedule bill payments, and enroll in automatic contribution plans for retirement accounts. Automating your finances reduces the likelihood of forgetting or procrastinating on important tasks.

4. **Live Below Your Means**: Practice living below your means by spending less than you earn and avoiding unnecessary debt. Cultivate a frugal mindset and prioritize saving and investing for the future over immediate gratification. Avoid lifestyle inflation and resist the temptation to overspend when your income increases. Consistently adhering to a modest lifestyle allows you to build wealth steadily over time.

5. **Stick to Your Budget**: Create a budget that reflects your financial goals and values, and commit to sticking to it consistently. Track your income and expenses, categorize your spending, and review your budget regularly to ensure you're staying on track. Make adjustments as needed to align your spending with your priorities and avoid overspending in discretionary categories.

6. **Practice Delayed Gratification**: Cultivate the habit of delaying gratification and making deliberate financial choices that prioritize long-term rewards over short-term pleasures. Avoid impulse purchases and unnecessary expenses by pausing to consider whether a purchase aligns with your goals and values. Practice patience and discipline in your spending habits to avoid unnecessary debt and maintain financial stability.

7. **Stay Focused on Your Why**: Remind yourself of the reasons behind your financial goals and the long-term benefits of staying

consistent and disciplined. Whether it's achieving financial independence, providing for your family, or realizing your dreams, keep your motivations front and center to stay focused and committed during challenging times. Visualize the future you're working towards and let it inspire you to stay disciplined in your financial habits.

8. **Seek Accountability and Support**: Surround yourself with accountability partners, mentors, or like-minded individuals who can support and encourage you on your financial journey. Share your goals and progress with trusted friends or family members, join online communities or forums, or work with a financial advisor or coach who can provide guidance, accountability, and encouragement as you work towards your goals.

By practicing consistency and discipline in your financial habits, you can make steady progress towards your goals, build wealth over time, and achieve the financial freedom and security you desire. Stay committed to your plan, remain adaptable in the face of challenges, and celebrate your achievements along the way as you create a brighter financial future for yourself and your loved ones.
Celebrating your financial victories is an important part of staying motivated and reinforcing positive financial habits. Here are some ways to reward yourself without breaking the bank:

1. **Plan Affordable Treats**: Treat yourself to small, affordable rewards that align with your financial goals. This could include enjoying a homemade meal at your favorite restaurant, treating yourself to a movie night at home, or indulging in a spa day using DIY treatments. Look for low-cost or free activities that bring you joy and relaxation without straining your budget.

2. **Enjoy Simple Pleasures**: Find joy in simple pleasures that don't require spending money. Take a walk in nature, spend quality time with loved ones, or curl up with a good book from the library. Engage in activities that nourish your soul and enhance

your well-being without adding financial stress.

3. **Celebrate Milestones Creatively**: Get creative with how you celebrate financial milestones. Host a potluck dinner with friends to celebrate paying off debt, organize a DIY craft night to commemorate reaching a savings goal, or plan a picnic in the park to mark a significant achievement. Focus on creating meaningful experiences and memories rather than spending money on lavish celebrations.

4. **Reward Yourself with Time**: Give yourself the gift of time as a reward for your financial achievements. Take a day off work to relax and recharge, schedule a staycation to explore your local area, or plan a weekend getaway to unwind and destress. Investing in self-care and relaxation can be a valuable reward that doesn't require spending a lot of money.

5. **Practice Gratitude**: Cultivate a mindset of gratitude and appreciation for your financial progress and accomplishments. Take time to reflect on how far you've come and acknowledge the hard work and dedication that led to your success. Express gratitude for the resources and support systems that have helped you along the way, whether it's friends, family, mentors, or your own resilience and determination.

6. **Set Non-Financial Rewards**: Consider setting non-financial rewards for reaching specific financial milestones. For example, reward yourself with a day off from household chores, permission to pursue a hobby or passion project guilt-free, or the opportunity to try a new activity or experience you've been curious about. Non-financial rewards can be just as rewarding and motivating as tangible gifts.

7. **Celebrate with Freebies and Discounts**: Take advantage of freebies, discounts, and rewards programs to celebrate your financial victories without spending money. Redeem loyalty points for a free meal or merchandise, use coupons or promo codes for discounted experiences, or participate in birthday

rewards offered by businesses and retailers. Look for ways to enjoy perks and benefits without paying full price.

8. **Share Your Successes with Others**: Celebrate your financial victories by sharing your successes with others and inspiring them on their own financial journeys. Share your story, lessons learned, and tips for success with friends, family, or online communities. Celebrating together creates a sense of camaraderie and support, and motivates others to pursue their own financial goals.

By finding creative and affordable ways to celebrate your financial victories, you can stay motivated, reinforce positive habits, and enjoy the journey towards financial success without sacrificing your budget or financial stability. Remember that celebrating doesn't have to be extravagant—it's the meaningful moments and small joys that matter most in the end.

Chapter 9: Passing Down Wealth Wisdom

Passing down wealth wisdom is about more than just leaving a financial inheritance—it's about imparting valuable knowledge, skills, and values to the next generation to help them navigate their own financial journeys successfully. In this chapter, we'll explore strategies for passing down wealth wisdom to future generations:

1. **Lead by Example**: One of the most powerful ways to teach wealth wisdom is by leading by example. Model responsible financial habits, such as budgeting, saving, investing, and living within your means, in your own life. Let your actions speak louder than words and demonstrate the importance of financial responsibility and stewardship.

2. **Start Early**: Begin teaching financial literacy and money management skills to children at an early age. Use everyday opportunities to teach concepts such as earning, saving, spending, and giving. Involve children in age-appropriate financial decisions and discussions, such as budgeting for family activities or saving for a special goal.

3. **Provide Financial Education**: Offer formal financial education and resources to children and young adults to help them develop a solid understanding of personal finance concepts. Teach them about budgeting, banking, credit, investing, taxes, and other financial topics relevant to their lives. Encourage them to ask questions, seek out information, and take ownership of their financial future.

4. **Set Up Financial Structures**: Establish financial structures such as trusts, custodial accounts, or education savings accounts to provide for the financial needs and aspirations of future generations. Work with legal and financial professionals to create a plan that aligns with your values and goals and ensures the

responsible management and distribution of wealth over time.

5. **Foster Entrepreneurship and Innovation**: Encourage creativity, entrepreneurship, and innovation among future generations by supporting their passions, interests, and entrepreneurial endeavors. Teach them the value of hard work, perseverance, and innovation in creating wealth and making a positive impact in the world. Instill an entrepreneurial mindset that values initiative, problem-solving, and adaptability.

6. **Promote Financial Independence**: Empower future generations to achieve financial independence and self-sufficiency by teaching them how to earn, manage, and grow their own wealth. Encourage them to pursue education, career opportunities, and entrepreneurial ventures that align with their interests and goals. Provide guidance and support as they navigate their own financial journeys and make important life decisions.

7. **Instill Values and Philanthropy**: Emphasize the importance of values such as integrity, generosity, and social responsibility in managing wealth and making financial decisions. Teach future generations about the joy and fulfillment that comes from giving back to others and making a positive impact in their communities and the world. Encourage them to engage in philanthropy and volunteerism as part of their financial legacy.

8. **Maintain Open Communication**: Foster open and honest communication about wealth, inheritance, and financial matters within your family. Create a supportive environment where family members feel comfortable discussing their financial goals, concerns, and aspirations. Share your own experiences, lessons learned, and values related to wealth management and stewardship.

9. **Lead Family Meetings and Discussions**: Organize family meetings and discussions to discuss financial matters, share updates on family wealth, and involve future generations in

decision-making processes. Use these meetings as opportunities to educate, inspire, and align family members around shared goals and values. Encourage collaboration, consensus-building, and mutual respect in managing family wealth.

10. **Document Family History and Values**: Preserve your family's history, values, and legacy for future generations by documenting important financial and non-financial aspects of your family's story. Create a family mission statement or legacy document that articulates your values, vision, and goals for future generations. Share stories, anecdotes, and lessons learned that illustrate your family's journey and collective wisdom.

By passing down wealth wisdom to future generations, you can empower them to make informed financial decisions, build wealth responsibly, and carry on your family's legacy for generations to come. Invest time, effort, and resources into educating and inspiring the next generation, knowing that the impact of your guidance and mentorship will extend far beyond your lifetime.

Teaching financial literacy to children and young adults is essential for equipping them with the knowledge, skills, and attitudes they need to make informed financial decisions and achieve financial well-being. Here are some strategies for effectively teaching financial literacy to children and young adults:

1. **Start Early**: Introduce basic financial concepts to children at an early age and build upon their understanding as they grow. Use age-appropriate language and activities to teach concepts such as earning money, saving, spending, budgeting, and giving. Encourage hands-on learning experiences that make financial concepts tangible and relevant to children's lives.

2. **Use Real-Life Examples**: Incorporate real-life examples and experiences into financial lessons to make them more meaningful

and relatable. Show children how money works in everyday situations, such as grocery shopping, paying bills, or saving for a goal. Use games, simulations, and role-playing exercises to teach financial concepts in a fun and engaging way.

3. **Lead by Example**: Model responsible financial behavior and attitudes in your own life to serve as a positive role model for children and young adults. Let them observe how you budget, save, invest, and make financial decisions. Use teachable moments to explain your thought process and involve them in age-appropriate financial discussions and activities.

4. **Encourage Saving and Goal Setting**: Teach children the importance of saving money and setting financial goals from a young age. Help them open a savings account and set aside money for short-term and long-term goals. Encourage them to track their progress, celebrate their achievements, and learn from setbacks along the way. Use visual aids such as charts or piggy banks to make saving tangible and rewarding.

5. **Introduce Banking Basics**: Teach children about basic banking concepts such as deposits, withdrawals, interest, and ATM usage. Take them on a tour of a bank branch to familiarize them with banking services and processes. Explain how to read a bank statement, balance a checkbook, and use online banking tools responsibly.

6. **Teach Budgeting Skills**: Introduce children to the concept of budgeting and help them create a simple budget that allocates money for different categories such as savings, spending, and giving. Teach them to differentiate between needs and wants, make informed spending choices, and prioritize their financial goals. Encourage them to review and adjust their budget regularly based on changing needs and circumstances.

7. **Explore Earning and Entrepreneurship**: Teach children about the value of work, entrepreneurship, and earning money through age-appropriate activities and discussions. Encourage

them to explore different ways to earn money, such as chores, allowances, or starting a small business. Teach them about the importance of hard work, initiative, and perseverance in achieving financial success.

8. **Introduce Investing Concepts**: As children mature, introduce them to basic investing concepts such as stocks, bonds, and mutual funds. Teach them about the power of compound interest, risk and return, and the importance of diversification. Start with simple investment vehicles such as a college savings plan or a custodial investment account and gradually expand their knowledge as they grow older.

9. **Address Credit and Debt**: Teach young adults about responsible credit and debt management to help them avoid common pitfalls and build a strong financial foundation. Explain how credit works, the importance of maintaining good credit, and the risks associated with excessive debt. Teach them to use credit cards responsibly, pay bills on time, and avoid high-interest debt whenever possible.

10. **Provide Ongoing Education and Support**: Offer ongoing financial education and support to children and young adults as they navigate their financial journey. Stay open to their questions, concerns, and learning needs, and provide guidance and resources to help them make informed decisions. Encourage them to seek out additional financial education opportunities, such as workshops, courses, or online resources, to deepen their understanding and skills.

By teaching financial literacy to children and young adults early and consistently, you empower them to make smart financial decisions, build wealth responsibly, and achieve financial independence and success in adulthood. Invest in their financial education and well-being, knowing that the knowledge and skills you impart will serve them well throughout their lives.

Inculcating healthy money mindsets and habits in the next generation is essential for their long-term financial well-being and success. Here are some strategies for instilling positive money attitudes and behaviors in children and young adults:

1. **Lead by Example**: Be a positive role model for the next generation by demonstrating healthy money habits and attitudes in your own life. Show them the importance of budgeting, saving, investing, and living within your means through your actions and decisions. Model responsible financial behavior and attitudes towards money, and explain the rationale behind your choices.

2. **Promote Financial Literacy**: Prioritize financial education and literacy as a fundamental skill for children and young adults. Teach them about basic financial concepts such as budgeting, saving, investing, debt management, and the value of compound interest. Provide age-appropriate resources, tools, and activities to help them develop a strong foundation of financial knowledge and skills.

3. **Encourage Critical Thinking**: Encourage children and young adults to think critically about money and financial decisions. Teach them to question advertising messages, compare prices, evaluate options, and consider the long-term consequences of their choices. Help them develop sound judgment and decision-making skills that empower them to make informed financial decisions.

4. **Foster a Growth Mindset**: Cultivate a growth mindset in children and young adults by emphasizing the importance of learning, growth, and resilience in achieving financial success. Encourage them to embrace challenges, learn from failures, and persist in the face of setbacks. Teach them that financial success is not determined by innate talent or luck, but by effort, persistence, and continuous improvement.

5. **Promote Delayed Gratification**: Teach children and young adults the value of delayed gratification and long-term thinking

in managing money. Encourage them to prioritize saving and investing for future goals over immediate spending on fleeting pleasures. Help them set meaningful goals, create action plans, and stay focused on their objectives despite temptations or distractions.

6. **Emphasize Needs vs. Wants**: Teach children and young adults to differentiate between needs and wants, and prioritize spending on essentials over discretionary purchases. Help them develop a sense of financial responsibility and self-discipline by encouraging thoughtful decision-making and self-control in their spending habits. Teach them to distinguish between short-term desires and long-term priorities in managing their money.

7. **Encourage Goal Setting**: Encourage children and young adults to set specific, achievable financial goals and create action plans to achieve them. Whether it's saving for a toy, a college education, or a dream vacation, teach them the importance of setting goals, making a plan, and taking consistent action to make their dreams a reality. Celebrate their successes and milestones along the way to reinforce positive behaviors.

8. **Teach the Value of Giving Back**: Instill the value of generosity and philanthropy in children and young adults by teaching them the importance of giving back to others. Encourage them to donate their time, talents, or money to causes they care about and make a positive impact in their communities. Teach them that true wealth is measured not only by what you have, but by what you give.

9. **Promote Financial Independence**: Empower children and young adults to take control of their own financial futures and become financially independent. Teach them the importance of earning, saving, and managing their own money from a young age. Encourage them to explore opportunities for entrepreneurship, innovation, and self-sufficiency that align with their interests and goals.

10. **Maintain Open Communication**: Foster open and honest communication about money within your family to create a supportive environment for learning and growth. Encourage children and young adults to ask questions, seek guidance, and share their financial goals and concerns. Be approachable, non-judgmental, and supportive in your conversations about money, and offer guidance and encouragement as needed.

By instilling healthy money mindsets and habits in the next generation, you empower them to make smart financial decisions, build wealth responsibly, and achieve financial independence and success in their lives. Invest time, effort, and resources into their financial education and well-being, knowing that the values and skills you impart will serve them well throughout their lives.

Leaving a legacy through estate planning and charitable giving is a meaningful way to make a positive impact and create a lasting legacy that extends beyond your lifetime. Here are some strategies for effectively planning your estate and incorporating charitable giving into your legacy:

1. **Define Your Legacy Goals**: Start by defining your legacy goals and values. What impact do you want to make on future generations and the world? Consider your personal values, passions, and priorities, as well as the causes and organizations you care about most. Your legacy goals will guide your estate planning and charitable giving decisions.

2. **Create a Comprehensive Estate Plan**: Work with legal and financial professionals to create a comprehensive estate plan that reflects your wishes and ensures the responsible management and distribution of your assets. This may include drafting a will, establishing trusts, designating beneficiaries, and creating powers of attorney and healthcare directives. Review and update your estate plan regularly to reflect changes in your circumstances or goals.

3. **Consider Tax Planning Strategies**: Explore tax planning strategies to minimize estate taxes and maximize the impact of your charitable giving. This may include gifting assets during your lifetime, establishing charitable trusts, utilizing donor-advised funds, or making strategic use of tax deductions and credits available for charitable contributions. Consult with tax advisors and estate planning professionals to develop a tax-efficient plan that aligns with your goals.

4. **Include Charitable Giving in Your Plan**: Incorporate charitable giving into your estate plan as a way to support causes and organizations that are meaningful to you. Consider allocating a portion of your assets, such as cash, securities, real estate, or personal property, to charitable beneficiaries through bequests, beneficiary designations, or charitable trusts. Choose charities and causes that align with your values and have a meaningful impact in areas such as education, healthcare, environmental conservation, or social justice.

5. **Establish a Family Foundation or Donor-Advised Fund**: Consider establishing a family foundation or donor-advised fund as a vehicle for charitable giving and philanthropy. These structures allow you to create a lasting legacy, involve family members in charitable decision-making, and support multiple charitable causes over time. Work with financial advisors and legal professionals to establish and manage these entities in accordance with applicable laws and regulations.

6. **Engage Family Members in the Process**: Involve family members in discussions about estate planning and charitable giving to ensure that your legacy reflects shared values and priorities. Encourage open communication, active participation, and collaboration in decision-making processes. Use family meetings and discussions to educate and inspire future generations about the importance of philanthropy and stewardship.

7. **Document Your Intentions and Values**: Document your intentions and values related to estate planning and charitable giving in a legacy letter, ethical will, or family mission statement. Share your personal stories, values, and aspirations with your loved ones to convey the meaning and purpose behind your legacy. Use these documents to articulate your wishes, express gratitude, and inspire future generations to carry on your legacy of generosity and impact.

8. **Educate and Empower Beneficiaries**: Educate and empower beneficiaries about their roles and responsibilities in managing and distributing your estate and charitable assets. Provide guidance and resources to help them fulfill their duties with integrity, transparency, and accountability. Encourage beneficiaries to honor your legacy by continuing to support charitable causes and make a positive impact in their communities.

9. **Plan for Succession and Continuity**: Plan for succession and continuity in managing family foundations, donor-advised funds, or other charitable entities to ensure their ongoing viability and effectiveness. Identify potential successors, mentors, or advisors who can carry on your legacy and uphold your values and vision for philanthropy. Develop governance structures, policies, and procedures to guide future generations in fulfilling their philanthropic responsibilities.

10. **Monitor and Evaluate Impact**: Monitor and evaluate the impact of your charitable giving over time to assess the effectiveness of your philanthropic efforts and ensure alignment with your legacy goals. Regularly review financial statements, grant reports, and program evaluations from charitable organizations to track progress, measure outcomes, and make informed decisions about future giving. Use feedback and data to refine your strategies, identify opportunities for improvement, and maximize the impact of your legacy.

By incorporating estate planning and charitable giving into your legacy, you can create a lasting impact that reflects your values, passions, and aspirations. By thoughtful planning, collaboration, and engagement with your loved ones and professional advisors, you can ensure that your legacy continues to make a positive difference in the lives of others for generations to come.

empowering others to take control of their finances, you contribute to a ripple effect of positive change that extends far beyond your immediate circle. Additionally, teaching reinforces your own understanding and helps you internalize key principles, deepening your own mastery of financial concepts.

In essence, the epilogue serves as a reminder that your financial journey is not just about personal gain—it's also about growth, contribution, and connection. By reflecting on your progress, committing to ongoing learning, and empowering others to achieve financial success, you not only enhance your own life but also contribute to a more financially empowered and resilient society as a whole.

Committing to lifelong learning and improvement is a mindset that acknowledges the ever-evolving nature of personal finance and the importance of staying informed, adaptable, and empowered throughout your financial journey. Here's why it's essential and how you can embrace it:

1. **Adapting to Change:** The financial landscape is constantly evolving, with new technologies, economic trends, and regulations shaping the way we manage money. By committing to lifelong learning, you can stay ahead of these changes and adapt your financial strategies accordingly. Whether it's understanding

how cryptocurrency works, navigating the gig economy, or optimizing your investments in a fluctuating market, ongoing education ensures you're equipped to handle whatever comes your way.

2. **Expanding Your Knowledge:** The more you know about personal finance, the better equipped you are to make informed decisions about your money. Lifelong learning allows you to deepen your understanding of financial concepts, from basic budgeting and saving techniques to advanced investment strategies and retirement planning. By expanding your knowledge base, you gain the confidence and competence to manage your finances effectively and achieve your goals.

3. **Building Financial Resilience:** Financial literacy is a key component of resilience, enabling you to navigate financial challenges and setbacks with confidence and resourcefulness. Lifelong learning equips you with the knowledge and skills to overcome obstacles, whether it's managing debt, coping with job loss, or weathering economic downturns. By continuously honing your financial literacy, you build resilience that helps you thrive in both good times and bad.

4. **Enhancing Decision-Making:** Financial decisions have far-reaching consequences that can impact your life for years to come. Lifelong learning improves your decision-making abilities by providing you with the information, tools, and insights needed to make sound financial choices. Whether it's weighing the pros and cons of a major purchase, evaluating investment opportunities, or planning for retirement, ongoing education empowers you to make decisions that align with your values and goals.

5. **Fostering Personal Growth:** Lifelong learning is about more than just acquiring knowledge—it's also a journey of personal growth and development. Engaging with new ideas, perspectives, and experiences fosters intellectual curiosity, critical thinking, and creativity. It challenges you to question assumptions, explore

alternatives, and expand your horizons beyond your comfort zone. By embracing lifelong learning, you cultivate a growth mindset that enhances your overall well-being and fulfillment.

To commit to lifelong learning and improvement in personal finance, consider the following strategies:

- **Set Learning Goals:** Define specific learning goals that align with your financial aspirations and areas of interest. Whether it's mastering a particular financial concept, exploring a new investment strategy, or obtaining a professional certification, setting goals gives you direction and motivation to pursue ongoing education.

- **Seek Diverse Learning Opportunities:** Take advantage of a wide range of learning opportunities, including books, articles, podcasts, online courses, workshops, seminars, and webinars. Explore reputable sources of financial information and seek out perspectives from diverse experts and practitioners. Be open to learning from different disciplines, such as psychology, economics, and behavioral finance, to gain insights into how people think and behave when it comes to money.

- **Stay Curious and Engaged:** Cultivate a curious and inquisitive mindset that drives your pursuit of knowledge and understanding. Stay curious about emerging trends, innovative technologies, and evolving best practices in personal finance. Engage actively with learning materials, ask questions, seek clarification, and participate in discussions to deepen your understanding and retention of key concepts.

- **Apply What You Learn:** Put your knowledge into practice by applying what you learn to real-life financial situations. Experiment with different strategies, tools, and techniques to see what works best for your unique circumstances. Reflect on your experiences, learn from both successes and failures, and use them as opportunities for growth and improvement.

- **Share Your Knowledge:** Share your expertise and insights with others by teaching, mentoring, or participating in financial education initiatives. By sharing your knowledge, you not only reinforce your own understanding of financial concepts but also contribute to the financial literacy and empowerment of others. Whether it's helping a friend create a budget, leading a financial literacy workshop, or volunteering with a nonprofit organization, find ways to give back and pay it forward.

By committing to lifelong learning and improvement in personal finance, you invest in your own financial well-being and empower yourself to achieve greater financial success and fulfillment. Embrace the journey of continuous learning as a lifelong pursuit that enriches your life, enhances your capabilities, and enables you to make a positive impact in the world around you.

"The Money Mastery" is a comprehensive handbook designed to empower readers with the knowledge, skills, and mindset needed to achieve financial success and independence. Through a series of chapters covering key aspects of personal finance, the book provides practical advice, actionable strategies, and insightful tips for managing money wisely and building wealth over time. Here's a summary of the main themes and topics covered in the book:

1. **Understanding Your Financial Landscape:** The book begins by helping readers assess their current financial situation, set clear goals, and identify their spending habits and patterns.

2. **Building a Solid Financial Foundation:** Readers learn how to create a realistic budget, establish an emergency fund, and debunk common money myths that may hinder their financial progress.

3. **Mastering Mindful Spending:** This section explores the importance of differentiating between needs and wants, practicing delayed gratification techniques, and utilizing budgeting apps and tools to track spending effectively.

4. **Maximizing Savings Through Smart Shopping:** Readers

discover strategies for finding the best deals, utilizing coupons, sales, and discounts, and avoiding impulse purchases that can derail their savings goals.

5. **Supercharging Savings with Frugal Living:** The book delves into the benefits of embracing minimalism, DIY practices, and repurposing/upcycling to save money and live more sustainably.

6. **Investing in Your Future:** Readers learn about different investment options, understanding risk and return, and starting small to build a diversified investment portfolio.

7. **Navigating Financial Challenges:** This section provides strategies for dealing with debt, overcoming financial hurdles like job loss or medical emergencies, and seeking professional help when needed.

8. **Cultivating Long-Term Financial Success:** The final chapters encourage readers to set and review financial milestones, practice consistency and discipline, celebrate victories, and pass down wealth wisdom to future generations.

Epilogue:

As you reach the conclusion of this journey through the "The Money Mastery," take a moment to reflect on the insights gained and the progress made on your path to financial empowerment. In this final chapter, we revisit the key themes and lessons learned, and look ahead to the future with optimism and purpose.

Reflecting on Your Journey:
Throughout this guide, you've embarked on a journey of self-discovery and empowerment, gaining valuable knowledge and skills to manage your finances effectively and build wealth for the future. Take pride in the progress you've made, from setting clear financial goals and creating a solid budget to making mindful spending choices and maximizing your savings. Celebrate the victories, no matter how small, and acknowledge the growth and transformation that have taken place along the way.

Committing to Lifelong Learning:
Your journey to financial freedom is not a destination, but a continuous process of learning and improvement. Commit to lifelong learning as a way to stay informed, adaptable, and empowered in your financial decisions. Explore new topics, seek out diverse perspectives, and embrace opportunities for personal growth and development. By cultivating a mindset of curiosity and openness, you can continue to evolve and thrive in an ever-changing financial landscape.

Empowering Others:
As you've gained wisdom and experience on your financial journey, consider how you can empower others to achieve their own financial goals. Share your knowledge, insights, and experiences with friends, family, and community members who may benefit from your guidance and support. Be a mentor, advocate, and role model for financial literacy and empowerment, especially among younger generations who are just beginning their financial journeys. By paying it forward and making a positive impact in the lives of others, you contribute to a more

financially resilient and prosperous society.

Looking Ahead:
As you close this chapter and embark on the next phase of your financial journey, remember that the principles and values you've learned here will continue to guide you along the way. Stay committed to your goals, remain adaptable in the face of challenges, and never stop learning and growing. With determination, resilience, and a sense of purpose, you can overcome obstacles, seize opportunities, and create the life of abundance and fulfillment you deserve.

Thank you for joining us on this journey through the "The Money Mastery." May your path to financial freedom be filled with prosperity, peace, and purpose.

Summary:

"The Money Mastery" is a comprehensive handbook designed to empower readers with the knowledge, skills, and mindset needed to achieve financial success and independence. The book covers a wide range of topics, including understanding your financial landscape, building a solid financial foundation, mastering mindful spending, maximizing savings through smart shopping, supercharging savings with frugal living, investing in your future, navigating financial challenges, and cultivating long-term financial success.

Throughout the book, readers are guided through practical advice, actionable strategies, and insightful tips to manage money wisely, save effectively, invest strategically, and overcome financial obstacles. Each chapter provides valuable insights and tools to help readers assess their current financial situation, set clear goals, and make informed decisions about budgeting, saving, spending, and investing.

The book emphasizes the importance of lifelong learning and personal growth, encouraging readers to stay curious, adaptable, and empowered in their financial journey. It also highlights the value of sharing knowledge and experiences with others, empowering readers to become mentors, advocates, and role models for financial literacy and empowerment in their communities.

www.ingramcontent.com/pod-product-compliance
Lightning Source LLC
Chambersburg PA
CBHW050327230526
45471CB00005B/2383